Dear Reader:

The book you are about to read is the latest bestseller from the St. Martin's True Crime Library, the imprint *The New York Times* calls "the leader in true crime!" Each month, we offer you a fascinating account of the latest, most sensational crime that has captured the national attention. St. Martin's is the publisher of bestselling true crime author and crime journalist Kieran Crowley, who explores the dark, deadly links between a prominent Manhattan surgeon and the disappearance of his wife fifteen years earlier in THE SURGEON'S WIFE. Suzy Spencer's BREAKING POINT guides readers through the tortuous twists and turns in the case of Andrea Yates, the Houston mother who drowned her five young children in the family's bathtub. In Edgar Award-nominated DARK DREAMS, legendary FBI profiler Roy Hazelwood and bestselling crime author Stephen G. Michaud shine light on the inner workings of America's most violent and depraved murderers. In the book you now hold, SECRETS IN THE CELLAR, acclaimed author John Glatt takes a closer look at the dark secrets of an Austrian family.

St. Martin's True Crime Library gives you the stories behind the headlines. Our authors take you right to the scene of the crime and into the minds of the most notorious murderers to show you what really makes them tick. St. Martin's True Crime Library paperbacks are better than the most terrifying thriller, because it's all true! The next time you want a crackling good read, make sure it's got the St. Martin's True Crime Library logo on the spine—you'll be up all night!

Charles E. Spicer, Jr.
Executive Editor, St. Martin's True Crime Library

SECRETS IN THE CELLAR

A True Story of the Austrian Incest Case
that Shocked the World

John Glatt

St. Martin's Paperbacks

CONTENTS

ACKNOWLEDGMENTS

I would like to thank Dr. Keith Ablow for his generous help with this project, as well as Dr. Laszlo Retsagi. Thanks also to Christa Woldrich, Trixi Mahd-Soltani, and Janina Alivio.

PROLOGUE

Vampire (as in "evil spirit") n. : (folklore) a corpse that rises at night to drink the blood of the living

April 2008

The call came in to Amstetten emergency services at precisely 7:00 a.m. that Saturday morning. An elderly man calmly informed the dispatcher that he had just discovered a young woman collapsed against a wall in his apartment building. She needed urgent medical help, he announced, giving the address Ybbsstrasse 40, before abruptly hanging up the phone.

The dispatcher immediately sent an ambulance and EMS crew to Ybbsstrasse, a busy main road near the center of the small Austrian town, 80 miles west of Vienna. There was little traffic that early on a weekend morning, and within minutes the medical crew had located the bedraggled young woman, lying unconscious on the doorstep. Her lip was covered in blood, where she had bitten her tongue, her skin was unnaturally pale and clumps of hair had been torn out of her head.

A few minutes later, the critically ill woman was admitted into the intensive care ward of the Mostviertel Amstetten-Mauer state hospital.

"She was in a life-threatening condition," recalled Dr. Albert Reiter, the head of the unit. "She was unconscious and had to be ventilated. Several of her vital organs had failed."

Three hours later, a silver Mercedes pulled into the hospital's parking lot, and a distinguished-looking gray-haired man with a bushy mustache got out. He walked briskly into the emergency room and introduced himself as Josef Fritzl, the grandfather of 19-year-old Kerstin, who had just been brought in by ambulance. He demanded to see a doctor immediately, saying he had an important note from the patient's mother about her condition.

"He was a very polite, very normal man," recalled Dr. Reiter, who met Fritzl in his office. "He was a correct man."

Fritzl explained he had been awakened by noises in the stairway of the building he owned. On further investigation, he had discovered the young woman, lying unconscious on his doorstep.

But there was more, he said, reaching for his jacket pocket. She had been clutching a handwritten note from his daughter Elisabeth, who had run away to join a religious sect twenty-four years earlier and not been seen since.

Then, handing the note to Dr. Reiter, he said this was the fourth child his wayward daughter had abandoned outside his house, for him and his wife to care for.

"Please, please help her," it read.

Wednesday, I gave her aspirin and cough medicine for the condition. Thursday, the cough worsened. Friday the coughing got even worse. She has been biting her lip as well as her tongue.

Kerstin is very scared of strangers. She has never been in a hospital before. I've asked my father for help, because he is the only person she knows.

At the bottom of the note, Elisabeth had added a postscript:

Kerstin, please stay strong, until we see each other again! We will come back to you soon!

Then the elderly man explained how, with each baby his daughter had deposited on his doorstep over the years, there was always a note, begging him to care for the baby, as her cult disapproved of children.

What else could he do under the circumstances? he asked Dr. Reiter, shrugging his shoulders. So he and his wife Rosemarie had brought up Elisabeth's three abandoned children, Lisa, 16, Monika, 15, and Alex, 12, as if they were their own.

When the bewildered doctor questioned Fritzl about his daughter's disappearance and whether he had tried to find her, the elderly man said he had to leave.

"I did not like his tone," remembered Dr. Reiter. "Something didn't seem right. He simply demanded we make Kerstin better, so he could take her away again."

Over the years, the head of the busy intensive care ward had seen thousands of emergency cases, but nothing compared to the apparent neglect suffered by Kerstin. On closer inspection, he was amazed to discover that the teenager was missing most of her teeth and had several large bald patches. Her skin was deathly white and she appeared to be severely anemic.

Initially, he thought she might have been poisoned, ordering immediate blood tests. But these came back negative. Then he speculated that she might be suffering from epilepsy. When the young girl's vital organs started to shut down, Dr. Reiter put her on life support.

The experienced doctor was puzzled and disturbed at how a mother could just abandon such a sick daughter on a doorstep before vanishing.

"From the tone of the letter," said Dr. Reiter, "it was clear that she cared very deeply for her child."

So at 10:37 a.m., he telephoned Amstetten police, reporting that he had admitted a mysterious female in critical condition, and they needed to investigate.

A few hours later, a policeman arrived at Ybbsstrasse 40 to interview Josef Fritzl about what had happened to his granddaughter. Amstetten police were well acquainted with how Elisabeth had run off in 1984, at the age of 18, to join a religious cult. Her worried parents had reported her missing at the time, and the local police, then Interpol, had all investigated. But she had disappeared without a trace, and there were no leads.

The following year, when Elisabeth turned 19, they'd stopped looking. She was no longer a minor under Austrian law, and was free to go wherever she liked.

At the house, her seemingly upright 73-year-old father told the officer about discovering Kerstin collapsed on his doorstep, bearing a note from her mother. He then produced three other notes his daughter had sent over the years, explaining that each one had accompanied a baby.

In January, he explained, Elisabeth had sent him a letter referring to Kerstin's medical problems. She had written that she would soon be coming home with her other children, Stefan, 18, and Felix, 5, to rejoin the family so they could all celebrate birthdays together.

Although Amstetten police didn't doubt Josef, a successful property speculator, they nevertheless re-opened the case of Elisabeth Fritzl, who was still officially classified after twenty-four years as "missing." Dr. Reiter had convinced them that knowledge of the mother's medical history was essential to diagnosing her mysterious illness, and saving her life.

The January letter bore a postmark from the town of Kematen an der Krems, 43 miles east of Amstetten, so that's where the search began. Over the next several days, investigators contacted all the nearby hospitals and schools for any information about Elisabeth, who would now be 42 years old. They also searched the central registry database and social security offices.

"Every avenue was explored," said Amstetten District Governor Hans-Heinz Lenze. "There wasn't a shred of evidence about Elisabeth."

On Monday morning—two days after Kerstin had been admitted to the hospital—investigators summoned Manfred Wohlfahrt, the officer in charge of sects for the nearby St. Polten diocese, to Amstetten police station. This was the first time he had ever been consulted about the case.

Wohlfahrt was asked to study Elisabeth's first letter, written soon after her disappearance, as well as the new one found on Kerstin. Did the two letters hold any clues to the sect she had joined, or her present whereabouts?

The expert thought the strangely stilted handwriting resembled "calligraphy." He also noted the unusual construction of the sentences, as if they had been "dictated." Later he would describe the notes as "odd" and "not very authentic." But he wasn't able to come to any conclusions about the sect or her whereabouts.

Back at the hospital, as Kerstin's condition worsened, she was put on dialysis, and a local priest was summoned to give last rites.

Dr. Reiter was becoming more and more frustrated at the lack of progress being made to find her mother.

"I was certain of only one thing," he said. "That the mother was the only one that could help."

So he telephoned Josef Fritzl, explaining the "desperate" situation, and how Elisabeth must be contacted to save Kerstin's life. Once again her father seemed evasive and uncooperative.

"I could not understand why he was so reluctant to help," said the doctor.

By Monday afternoon, Dr. Reiter decided to take matters into his own hands. He instructed the hospital's public relations department to issue a press release, appealing for Elisabeth to come forward, giving his personal mobile phone number as a contact hotline. Then he made another call to Josef Fritzl, somehow persuading him to supply an old photograph of Elisabeth for the media.

That night the doctor appeared on the Austrian ORF television news and made a plea to the public.

"I would like the mother to contact us," he replied. "We'll treat the contact with high discretion and will probably get a step further in our diagnosis and treatment."

The following day, when several journalists arrived at Josef Fritzl's house for an interview, they found him strangely hostile, as he ordered them off his property.

"I asked him for a photo of his daughter," recalled reporter Andrea Kramer of the *Osterreich* newspaper. "He was really aggressive and wanted to chase me away. He said he would help himself and didn't need help from anyone else."

Another journalist was also "shocked" by his surprising response.

"Instead of being the concerned father I expected," she said, "he told me to clear off. He said he wanted nothing to do with the appeal, but that the 'bloody doctor' had forced him into it."

By Wednesday, April 23, still with no leads, Amstetten police changed tack, concentrating their efforts on the Fritzl family. They arrived at Ybbsstrasse 40 to take DNA samples from Josef and Rosemarie Fritzl, as well as Lisa, Monika, and Alexander—the children Elisabeth had abandoned, whom the Fritzls were bringing up.

Investigators reasoned that since she had given birth to the children in a sect, there might be more than one father, one of whom might have a criminal record and be traceable.

"Herr Fritzl didn't have time to give a DNA sample," said the chief investigator, Inspector Franz Polzer, "and kept postponing, because he had so much to do."

The following Saturday evening—one week after Kerstin had been found—Josef called Dr. Reiter with astonishing news.

"Elisabeth has returned," he announced triumphantly. "I am bringing her to the hospital and she wants to see her daughter."

He urged the doctor not to call the police, saying he and Elisabeth "do not want any trouble."

Half an hour later, a disoriented woman with snow-white hair weakly shuffled up to the reception desk at the hospital, asking for Dr. Reiter.

"I am Kerstin's mother," she said. "I am here to help my daughter."

* * *

After nervously talking to Dr. Reiter for a few minutes about Kerstin's medical problems, Elisabeth said she had to go and meet her father, who was waiting for her outside. Soon afterward, Amstetten police, having been tipped off by Dr. Reiter, picked them both up for questioning.

They first interviewed Elisabeth, still believed to be a dangerously irresponsible mother. Initially she stuck to her father's story that she was a runaway who had joined a sect as a teenager and been there ever since. But slowly, under the investigators' persistent questioning, her credibility began to fall apart.

Finally, she took a deep breath and said she would tell them the truth. But first they had to promise to protect her, her mother and her children, and that she would never have to see her father again.

After they'd agreed, the 42-year-old woman broke down in tears, telling how her father Josef Fritzl had started raping her when she was 11. Then, on August 28, 1984, he had drugged her and locked her up in a dungeon under their home, beating her mercilessly and making her his sex slave. Since then, she had given birth to seven of his children, one of them dying at just three days old because of medical neglect.

And tonight, she told the astonished detectives, was the very first time she had ever been outside that underground dungeon in twenty-four years.

CHAPTER 1

A Nazi Childhood

Josef Stefan Fritzl was born in Amstetten, Lower Austria, on April 9, 1935, amidst the early rumblings of political upheaval from the rise of Nazism in neighboring Germany. His mother, Maria, a devout Roman Catholic, ruled the family, totally dominating his father, Josef Sr., a poor laborer with few ambitions.

The highly intelligent only child grew up in a climate of cruel uncertainty and discipline, both inside the Fritzl home and out.

Although the scenic mountainous region was settled in the Stone Age, the first known written mention of Amstetten was in 1111. The most notable event in its thin history was the Battle of Amstetten in November 1805, when Napoleon's army overran the town, killing hundreds of Austrian soldiers. Then in 1858, the railroad came to Amstetten, linking it to the rest of the Austria–Hungarian Empire.

Today's Amstetten is a small nondescript market town, lying midway between Vienna and Linz. It reclines in a valley of rolling green hills, noted for its apple cider and pear perry, with picturesque mountains and ancient fairy-tale castles towering in the distance. Indeed, the good climate and scenic views conjure up idyllic images of *The Sound of Music*, something the Austrian tourist board still trades on.

But when Josef Fritzl was growing up there in the late 1930s, there were dark clouds on the horizon that would help shape his later life.

On March 13, 1938, less than a month before his third birthday, the Austrian Nazi Party proclaimed the Anschluss, or union, were inviting the new German Chancellor Adolf Hitler to occupy Austria. The next day the Führer, who had been born less than ninety miles from Amstetten, made a triumphant visit to the small town, to the ecstatic cheers of the adoring townspeople.

Maria Fritzl and her little son Josef were among the delighted throng saluting Hitler as he ceremoniously drove around the main square in an open car.

"The crowd were screaming and waving," read a report in a local history book.

Later, Hitler personally thanked Amstetten in a letter, writing how his visit had "filled him with great pleasure," and thanking the city council for making him an honorary citizen.

One year later, Maria Fritzl threw her husband out of their small apartment for philandering, eventually divorcing him. Josef Sr. was reportedly killed in the war years later, fighting as a Nazi storm trooper, his name inscribed on a war memorial in the town square.

Little Josef grew up despising his father, considering him a "loser," though he idolized his mother, feeling she was the embodiment of the perfect woman. But Maria Fritzl was by all accounts an eccentric and strange woman, valuing discipline above everything else, in line with the ideology of the Third Reich. She reportedly encouraged her son to join the Hitler Youth movement after the war began, to make a man of him.

It was a violent childhood for little Josef, and he

would be beaten regularly by his mother, whom he would later accuse of waiting years to have him treated for a painful urinary-tract infection.

"He grew up without a father," said his future sister-in-law Christine R., "and his mother raised him with her fist, beating him until he was black and blue almost every day."

Years later, he would speak about his mother's extreme brutality.

"She used to beat me," he remembered, "hit me until I was lying in a pool of blood on the floor. It left me feeling totally humiliated and weak. I never had a kiss from her . . . she kept insulting me and told me I was a Satan, a criminal, a no-good. The only thing she ever did with me was to go to the church."

Life for both the Fritzls was filled with hardship. In those days, divorce in the ultra-conservative Roman Catholic town was scandalous. And they were so poor, they often relied on the charity of neighbors so they wouldn't starve.

In June 1941, when Germany invaded the Soviet Union, Amstetten became a vital strategic railhead for German troops leaving to fight on the eastern front, and 6-year-old Josef grew accustomed to seeing German soldiers walking through the streets, or waiting for train connections. There were thousands of SS troops stationed there, enthusiastically patronizing the local bars and brothels, where they were welcomed like heroes.

Years later Josef Fritzl would admit that this early exposure to Nazism exerted a strong and lasting influence on him, instilling a lifelong respect for control and authority.

Soon after the war started, he enrolled at the local elementary school in Amstetten, immediately impressing teachers with his keen intelligence and ordered mind. He was always well-behaved and popular with his school friends, who nicknamed him "Sepp" ("Pepper").

Throughout the war, Amstetten would be a strategic target for the Allies. So the little boy spent many nights with his mother in a shelter, as RAF planes repeatedly bombed the main railway line linking Vienna and Linz. Later there would be much speculation that Maria Fritzl had sexually molested her young son over this turbulent period, as bombs were falling over Amstetten. Perhaps he had felt trapped and disempowered, as his controlling mother crossed the boundaries into incest. Whatever happened between them sexually would scar the little boy for life, with disastrous results.

Just a short walk from their tiny one-room apartment was the Mauer clinic, part of the notorious Mauthausen–Gusen concentration camp network. The Nazis had built the stately camp in Amstetten at the outbreak of war, ultimately killing hundreds of patients in line with the Third Reich's euthanasia laws.

A further eight hundred men and women worked railroad construction at the main Amstetten terminus, before being transported to other camps for execution.

After the war, the Amstetten town council commissioned a book entitled *Amstetten 1938–1945*, which included a chapter on the wartime atrocities committed at the Mauer clinic against "unworthy lives." It listed 346 cases of patients being executed as part of the Mauer's 1941 euthanasia program, mainly concentrating on psychiatric and elderly patients.

"The first step to eliminating inherited and mental diseases was sterilization," the book states. "The last was euthanasia."

At the end of the war, the notoriously sadistic Nazi psychiatrist Dr. Emil Gelny visited the clinic. A fanatical member of the Nazi Party since 1933, Dr. Gelny

had invented "electro-executions," a barbaric procedure where four electrodes were attached to the patient's hands and feet. Then a high voltage current was
run through them until they died in agony—which
could take up to ten minutes.

During his 1944 visit, Dr. Gelny amused himself by
selecting thirty-nine "unnecessary mouths," then killing them with various drugs, including morphine, Ve-
ronal and Luminal. After the war, he escaped to Syria
and then Iraq, where he practiced medicine in Baghdad
until his death in 1961.

The evil Mauer death camp permeated Amstetten
during the war, and little Sepp Fritzl knew it well. He
grew up in its shadow, seeing inmates wearing their
distinctive uniforms lined up at the terminus every day
on his way to school.

The little boy was intrigued by the Mauer camp,
which held a strange fascination for him.

In May 1945, a month after Fritzl's tenth birthday, U.S.
troops liberated Amstetten. Soon the Soviet Red Army
would follow in their wake, occupying Austria for the
next decade. Sepp Fritzl would have witnessed the com-
munist invasion first-hand, living through the extended
occupation, notorious for the many rapes of Austrian
women.

The war took a terrible toll on Amstetten, which had
almost been destroyed by Allied attacks. It was a dan-
gerous place, with many unexploded bombs, especially
around the train station. Sepp Fritzl and his friends often played soccer in the streets among the bombed-out
ruins.

He and his mother lived in a poor neighborhood,
and soccer was considered the only escape. It was said
that whoever owned a leather football ruled the street

like a kaiser, with the ragged neighborhood children prizing dribbling skills above everything else.

But in these years, Sepp Fritzl was something of a loner, possessing few soccer skills. Although he was handsome, with jet-black hair and piercing blue eyes, he hardly stood out from the other boys, who often shunned him.

Years later he would claim to have survived his miserable childhood by reading any books he could lay his hands on. It was at this time that he realized he was highly intelligent, and found confidence.

In 1947, Josef Fritzl started at Amstetten Secondary Sports School, where he would spend the next four years. Former classmates still remember the 12-year-old as "slightly different," with an "unfashionable haircut" that his mother had given him to save money.

Andreas P., who grew up on the same street as the Fritzls, remembers Maria Fritzl as a "mysterious" woman, unable to tolerate daylight.

"She always put her hands over her forehead and eyes," he said. "She was very sensitive to light."

By his own admission, Fritzl worshiped his mother, who had by this time found a job, somewhat raising their standard of living. He later lauded her as "the best woman in the world," who'd taught him the values he would live by.

Even though she often beat him mercilessly, he believed it was for his own good and a necessary preparation for adult life.

Years later he would describe himself as an "alibi child," claiming his mother only had him to prove to his father that she was not sterile. He would also talk of having an "evil streak" that he was born with and fought against his entire life.

Josef Fritzl would also deny any sexual relationship

with his mother, although he would admit harboring unfulfilled sexual fantasies toward her. He would talk of loving her "across all boundaries," strangely congratulating himself for resisting his strong urges to consummate their relationship.

"It's complete rubbish to say my mother sexually abused me," he would tell an Austrian newspaper in 2008. "I suppose you could describe me as her man, sort of . . . She was the boss at home and I was the only man in the house."

At Amstetten Secondary Sports School, Fritzl initially had difficulties with his studies, but his work improved drastically after a teacher praised him and began taking an interest in the intelligent boy. He gained the reputation of a good student who never got into trouble.

On June 11, 1951, his class, 4B, went on a school trip to the Hellbrunn Residence, a few miles outside Salzburg. The class spent the day touring the stately 16th-century country residence of Prince-Archbishop Markus Sitticus.

Later, the handsome 16-year-old, dressed in traditional short pants and knickerbockers, was photographed with his classmates, posing by a statue for a souvenir picture. Josef Fritzl wore a blank enigmatic stare, his mouth registering neither a frown nor a smile. It is a youthful face bursting with strange dark secrets, way beyond its years.

CHAPTER 2

Starting a Family

A few weeks later, Josef Fritzl graduated from school, enrolling at a polytechnic for a one-year electrical engineering course. Then, after sailing through his final exams, he found a good job in Linz, 40 miles west of Amstetten, moving there with his mother.

The third largest city in Austria, Linz was far less parochial than Amstetten. The provincial capital of Upper Austria, it had been a thriving port on the Danube River during the Middle Ages. In the early 20th century, when the first Austrian railroad was built, Linz prospered from being a port on a direct rail line linking the Adriatic and Baltic Seas.

Adolf Hitler spent most of his childhood in Linz, studying at the Realschule. During his rise to power, he had envisioned it as an important cultural center for the Third Reich, and, a few hours after his 1938 Amstetten visit, had delivered a stirring speech from the Linz town hall, proclaiming the glorious union of Austria and Germany.

That same year the Fuhrer initiated a program to industrialize Linz, by moving in blast furnaces and steel factories from Czechoslovakia. The Hermann Göring Werke, or the VOEST company, manufactured steel, driving the Nazi war machine. After defeat in

1946, it became known as the United Austrian Iron and Steelworks, before being nationalized.

In 1951, 16-year-old Josef Fritzl started his first job at VOEST, soon gaining a reputation as a hard-working and brilliant engineer. Over the next several years, Fritzl spent his days working at the factory, before returning home to his mother.

As he entered his twenties, he was becoming something of a dandy, with a perfectly manicured mustache and expensive clothes. He frequented bars, and was popular with the girls, although he rarely went out with any, fearing his mother's disapproval.

It was around this time that he began exposing himself to women around the woods of Linz, finding a perverse thrill in the power it gave him over them. Late at night he would pedal his bicycle around the streets, spying on women, satisfying something growing deep inside him that he would later describe as "a volcano" he could barely control.

Over the next few years, the young exhibitionist would start attracting the attention of the Linz police with his unusual late-night activities.

In 1956, 21-year-old Josef Fritzl moved back to Amstetten, laying down the foundations of a new life that he could control completely. He selected a pretty 17-year-old local girl named Rosemarie for marriage. A barely educated, naïve girl who was nowhere near his intellectual match, Rosemarie, he felt, would be perfect to allow him to live the dissolute life he had in mind.

He had cunningly chosen her for her submissiveness and his ability to control her in the relationship—the total opposite of his manipulative mother.

Rosemarie, in turn, was attracted by some powerful quality she saw in him, for she would remain with him for more than half a century, allowing herself to be ruthlessly dominated without complaint.

Fritzl immediately announced his intention to raise a large family, for the power and prestige he felt it would give him. His naturally nurturing new wife was . only too happy to oblige.

Soon after they married, Rosemarie became pregnant. In 1958, their daughter Ulrike was born, the first of seven children Rosemarie would bear him over the next thirteen years. Josef would make his young wife bring them up, doing nothing except disciplining them with his fist.

From the beginning, Rosemarie's family distrusted Josef Fritzl, believing he was cruel and exploitative.

"I always hated him," said her younger sister Christine. "When Rosemarie married Josef, she was only seventeen. She was at his mercy."

One year later, the new father was arrested after a Linz woman complained that he had exposed himself to her.

"We recorded Fritzl as an exhibitionist," who'd already acquired a police record by this time, recalled now-retired Linz Police Chief Gerhard Marwan. A local newspaper report at the time described Fritzl as being "no stranger to the Linz police," with "two other relevant offenses, once for exhibitionism, and the other time for attempted rape."

But his arrest for indecency did not appear to bother Rosemarie, by now pregnant with their second child Rosemarie who was born in 1960.

There are few records of Josef Fritzl's life over the next several years, but he would later boast of leaving his wife and children behind in Amstetten, while he spent three years in Ghana, working on radio installations.

"I had various short flings with women in Ghana," he would later boast. "Nothing serious. I was worried about sexually transmitted diseases. I always chose nice girls, no prostitutes, for that reason."

By early 1963, he was back in Amstetten with Rosemarie, who later that year gave birth to their first son Harald. Josef was also commuting to Linz, where he had been rehired at the VOEST steelworks.

Most work nights, Fritzl slept over at the Linz home of Rosemarie's parents, Franz and Rosa, often arriving home in the early hours of the morning after spending the night spying on women. The mere act of exposing himself no longer satisfied his growing dark sexual fantasies.

"He was a voyeur," one of his unfortunate victims would later tell police. "He used to ride around on his bicycle and watch everyone."

On April 16, 1966, Rosemarie Fritzl gave birth to their fourth child, Elisabeth. She was a beautiful, affectionate baby, and from the very beginning, her father felt a strange attraction to her.

He became obsessed with her as a toddler, calling her "Liesel." He loved her thick red hair, classic high cheekbones, piercing eyes and angelic smile. Later he would say she reminded him physically of his mother.

As she flowered into the most beautiful of his eventual four daughters, he began lusting after her.

To all appearances, Josef Fritzl was a hard-working respectable family man, going places. He took his wife and children to the local church every Sunday, and all their neighbors considered the handsome, immaculately groomed engineer and his attractive wife to be model parents.

But Fritzl was a chimera and his moods could change

without warning. Behind closed doors, he ruled his family like a dictator, expecting everyone to abide by his strict set of rules. If they didn't, he would lash out with his fists.

"He was such a tyrant," remembered his sister-in-law Christine. "When he said it was black, it was black. When it was ten times white, it was black for him. He tolerated no dissent."

Four months after Elisabeth was born, a 17-year-old girl named Anna Neumayr disappeared on her way to Wels, a small village just 18 miles away from Linz. Three days later, on August 25, 1966, her body was found in a cornfield near her home in Pfaffstaett bei Mattinghofen in Lower Austria. She had been shot twice in the head by a captive bolt pistol, commonly used to slaughter livestock. At the time, homicide detectives viewed it as a particularly violent sex crime.

Anna's murderer was never caught, and it would be another forty-two years until Josef Fritzl, who was well acquainted with the area, would be questioned by police about the murder.

CHAPTER 3

"If You Scream, I Will Kill You!"

By summer 1967, Josef Fritzl was losing control as his insatiable sex drive was making him take more and more risks. He now spent hours hiding in the bushes, spying on women, leading to a rash of complaints to the police about his perverse behavior.

Then on September 4, police say he turned violent, attempting to drag a young woman into the Linz-Ebels woods and rape her. She fought him off, managing to escape. Several weeks later, he struck again, allegedly raping a 20-year-old Linz woman. His terrified victim was "too embarrassed" to go to the police, remaining silent for the next forty years.

Four weeks later on October 6, Josef Fritzl climbed through the kitchen window of another woman's home after midnight. He took a large knife from a drawer, wrapping it in a dishcloth, before sneaking into the bedroom. Then, at knifepoint, he violently raped a newly married 24-year-old nurse in her bed, while her husband was away, working the night shift.

"I felt the bedclothes being pulled back," the woman would tell an Austrian newspaper in 2008, still too traumatized to give her real name. "At first I thought it was my husband coming home, but then I felt this knife being pushed against my throat. He pushed it against my neck and said, 'If you scream, I will kill you.' Then he raped me. I will never forget those eyes."

As Josef Fritzl calmly walked out of the bedroom, he threatened to return and kill her if she ever told anyone what had happened.

Three weeks later, Linz police arrested Fritzl for the rape, and under interrogation, he broke down and confessed.

"We traced him by a print from his palm at the scene," recalled Gerhard Marwan. "He was identified by the victim, a nurse, as well as by a twenty-one-year-old woman who was attacked in Ebelsbergerwald woods, but managed to escape."

The official police report for the incident read:

On October 24, 1967, the engineer Josef Fritzl, 32, was questioned and arrested, after he managed to enter the bedroom of a flat on the raised ground floor belonging to a 24-year-old married nurse on the night of October 6, 1967, threatening her with a knife and raping her. Already on September 4, 1967, in Linz-Ebels he tried to drag a passing-by 21-year-old woman into the woods and rape her.

The local daily newspaper, *Oberösterreichische Nachrichten*, reported Fritzl's arrest, in a story headlined "Father of Four Exposed by Police as Vulgar Sex Offender. Came Through the Window—Threatened Woman With Death."

After his rape arrest, Fritzl was fired from his job at VOEST, and a few months later a Linz court sentenced him to 18 months' imprisonment.

"I was sixteen when he was locked up," remembered his sister-in-law Christine. "And I found the crime simply disgusting, not least because he already had four children with my sister. I deeply despised him for that. He was born a criminal and he will die a criminal."

In 2008, when asked why he had raped the young nurse, Fritzl replied, "I do not know what drove me to do that. I always wanted to be a good husband and a good father."

During his 18 months' incarceration, Rosemarie Fritzl stood by her husband, ignoring her family's pleas to take their four children and walk out on him. The story had been well publicized in the newspapers, and everyone in Amstetten was aware of it. But Rosemarie Fritzl carried on as if nothing had happened, her head held high.

"Everyone makes a mistake," said Christine. "She tried to hold the family together as well as possible. I think this changed their relationship a little. You can surely imagine that a woman in such a situation would have been utterly broken and shocked over something like this."

On Josef Fritzl's release from prison in late 1969, the talented engineer had few problems finding a new job. He was immediately hired by the Amstetten construction company Zehnter Baustoffhandel und Betonwerk, who apparently turned a blind eye to putting a convicted rapist on the payroll.

"My father often said he was an absolute genius," remembered Sigrid Reisinger, whose late father had hired him and who now runs the company. "He was hired even though he had a record of a sexual nature."

But other employees at the company, which manufactures construction materials, were less comfortable with the prospect of working alongside a sex offender.

"I didn't want that," a former female employee later

told a German newspaper, saying she repeatedly warned her children to avoid any contact with him.

Nevertheless, the industrious Josef Fritzl gained a reputation as a brilliant technician, and was on the fast track to promotion. He was soon appointed technical director, overseeing a complicated project to develop machinery for the manufacture of concrete sewage pipes.

The massive pipes were sixteen-and-a-half feet tall, ten feet wide and ten feet deep. The research and development project took Fritzl and his team many months to finish, teaching him invaluable lessons in pouring concrete and construction methods.

"Concrete technology was Fritzl's specialty," explained Franz Halder, who spent three months as his project assistant. "He could have built anything."

At work, Josef Fritzl refused to discuss his private life, keeping to himself. In all the time they spent together, all Halder knew about his boss was that he was married and had a criminal record.

"He did an excellent job," another employee would later tell the London *Times*, "but there was always something uneasy about him, as it was widely known that he had served time in prison for a sexual offense."

When Josef Fritzl turned 35 in April 1970, it appeared as though prison had finally taught him to control his obsessive sexual cravings. But that was far from the case. The only lesson he had learned was to be more careful—and to never get caught again.

In 1971, a year after Josef's release, Rosemarie Fritzl became pregnant again, giving birth to twins, Josef Jr. and Gabrielle. Now a father of six, Josef Fritzl decided his family needed more room, moving into his mother's large three-level house in the thriving Ybbsstrasse, a main shopping thoroughfare in Amstetten.

When he moved into the house, he told neighbors that Maria Fritzl had died, but he would later claim to have imprisoned her in a top floor bedroom until she finally died in 1980.

"I locked her up in a room at the top of the house," he reportedly confessed to a psychiatrist. "I then bricked in the window so that she never again saw the light of day."

Built in 1890, number 40 was a drab gray provincial house, just a few blocks from where he had been raised. It was on a busy main road lined with cafes, with a bakery next door, and a flower store and tattoo parlor across the street. It was also not overlooked by any neighboring homes—something he took into account when purchasing it.

Just a ten-minute walk away was the immaculately groomed town's main square, with its smart yellow-and-white painted town hall. A large golden spread eagle peered out over the town, dominating the landscape and watching the 23,000 residents.

Josef Fritzl had decided to become an entrepreneur, viewing his mother's house as a business investment. He first demolished the original house, then built a new one a few yards nearer to the road.

But he was careful to leave the small cellar beneath the old house intact—for he already had ambitious plans to develop it into a private bunker, where he could do what he wanted without any inquiring eyes to see.

It was common knowledge in Amstetten that Fritzl was a convicted sex offender. By nature Austrians mind their own business and respect privacy. However, some nearby residents quietly warned their children to keep away from Ybbsstrasse 40.

"I was only ten at the time," recalled one former

neighbor, "but I remember how we children were afraid to play near [his] house, because of the rumors that he had raped a woman and spent some time in jail for it."

Soon after his twins were born, Josef Fritzl took a new job for a German company, selling industrial machines all over Austria. He bought a new Mercedes and began dressing immaculately in suits. He was by all accounts a highly persuasive and successful salesman.

His new job also meant being away from his wife and family for several days at a time. He began frequenting many of Lower Austria's brothels, developing a taste for sadomasochistic sex. But his sexual demands were now so extreme that many prostitutes were too scared to take him as a customer.

Back at home, Josef Fritzl terrorized his family. He ran his new house like military boot camp, insisting his children always call him "sir." He also imposed strict curfews, demanding they come straight home from school. If they ever disobeyed his edicts, he would beat them with his fist until they were black and blue, just like his mother had done to him.

"He behaved like a drill instructor with his children," said his sister-in-law Christine. "They had to stop whatever they were doing and stand still when he would enter the room—even if they were in the middle of some game. You could sense their constant fear of punishment."

And he did not spare his wife Rosemarie from his violent temper; she often feared for her life.

"Josef beat her, and she was petrified of him," said her friend Anton Klammer. "Rosemarie was happy and normal, but when he was around she used to shrink away."

Christine said her older sister was totally "dominated and constantly belittled in public" by her husband, never daring to answer him back.

"If she had," said Christine, "we don't know what he would have done to her. Maybe he would have slapped her. In any case, he was a tyrant. What he said was good and the others had to shut up."

In late 1972, Rosemarie, now 33, became pregnant for the seventh and final time. Many in Amstetten had forgotten Josef's criminal past, now considering him the image of a good Catholic father. They respected his work ethic and dedication to his family, even if he was an old-school disciplinarian. At that time in Austria, the physical punishment of children was well accepted, even thought to be a necessary part of good child rearing.

In 1973, Josef Fritzl branched out into the hospitality business, buying an inn and leasing a nearby campsite on the banks of the scenic Mondsee Lake in Upper Austria. Lying 92 miles west of Amstetten, the breathtakingly beautiful Mondsee (Moon) is one of Austria's premier tourist resorts.

Each year, thousands of visitors arrive to see the imposing Drachenwand and Schafberg Mountains, towering majestically over the freshwater lake. And no trip there is complete without visiting a nearby church, where the famous *Sound of Music* wedding scene was filmed.

Seven miles long and one mile wide, Mondsee Lake resembles a crescent moon—which is how it got its name.

According to legend, a Bavarian duke was saved from drowning in the lake by the light of a full moon. He later founded the Mondsee monastery as a thank you. In summer the lake's water is said to be warmer than any other Austrian lake, making it a popular spot for swimming and sailing.

Josef Fritzl, who was a keen fisherman, was also

drawn there by the excellent fishing, as the lake is rich with a variety of marine life, including three different types of trout, as well as carp, whitefish and burbot.

He had quit his job as a salesman to devote himself full-time to property development, ordering Rosemarie to run the guest house—which he had christened "Seestern" (Starfish).

But first he worked hard, landscaping the campsite and renovating the guest house to prepare for its first customers. The residents of Unterach, the tiny town by the lake, were most impressed by Josef Fritzl's professionalism.

"He was an upright gentleman who was never out of line," Unterach City Council member Helmut Greifeneder later told the German magazine *Stern*. "He wanted strict order, and when he made contracts he made sure every word was perfect."

Fritzl's new campsite was laid out immaculately. All the caravans were lined up perfectly in formation, on a manicured lawn with perfectly landscaped flowerbeds.

Businessman Anton Graf, who rented land to Fritzl, said his tenant was a man of his word and totally reliable.

"We had a business relationship," Graf recalled. "He was correct. If he borrowed a tool and said he would return it two days later, then two days later, it was back. If he gave you his word, you could count on it."

Every summer, Fritzl remained in Amstetten with the children, while Rosemarie ran the guest house with a skeleton staff. For the next few years, this continued, Rosemarie only too glad to steer clear of her ruthlessly dominating husband, who had announced after the birth of their daughter Doris that year that he had no further use for her sexually, as she had gained weight.

But the father of seven wanted more children, and had already selected a second wife to start a new family with.

Soon after leasing the camping ground, Josef Fritzl became good friends with Paul Hoerer and his girlfriend Andrea Schmitt, a young couple from Munich, Germany, who spent a 1973 camping vacation at Mondsee Lake. Over the next thirty-five years, Hoerer and Schmitt would get to know Fritzl and his family well.

"We spent a lot of time together after that," said Hoerer. "When we first met Josef, he was a really kind, outgoing and open-minded person who laughed a lot. Josef, Rosemarie, Andrea and I always had so much fun—we laughed all the time."

The couple would visit the Fritzls' Amstetten home, meeting Rosemarie and their children numerous times over the years. Paul spent memorable nights with Josef and Rosemarie, dining on the elaborate roof terrace Fritzl had designed and built.

"[He] was a decent, outgoing and, above all, amusing bloke," said Hoerer. "[His house was] tip-top. White marble everywhere."

When they entertained guests, Rosemarie always played the part of a happily married wife—but that was far from the truth.

In the early 1970s, she became best friends with Elfriede Hoera, who worked for three summers in the kitchen at the Fritzls' guest house. Years later, Elfriede would recall how Rosemarie had confided to her that "Fritzl was a tyrant who terrorized his family. He bossed them around and brutalized them like an army officer. She stayed in the marriage because of the kids. Many times she told me that she was afraid to stand up to him, for fear of being beaten up." She said if she ran away, he would only track her down and make her life hell.

In 1974, there was a serious fire at the Seestern guest house, and police suspected it was arson. Josef Fritzl was brought in for questioning by Unterach investigators, but later released, as there was not enough evidence to charge him.

Over the next few years there would be several more suspicious fires at his Mondsee Lake property, with Fritzl collecting thousands of dollars in insurance claims.

CHAPTER 4

Elisabeth

In 1975, Josef Fritzl and his family attended a christening. A photograph taken there shows 9-year-old Elisabeth wearing a pink V-neck suit, with a fashionably peaked rainbow hat. Next to her sits her elder brother Harald, her closest and most trusted sibling. Two seats away is her father, wearing a smart blue suit and kipper tie, a broad smile on his craggy face. It appears to be a perfect Kodak moment for a perfect family.

The Fritzl patriarch was a sentimental man, making a point of attending family reunions and holiday celebrations with his wife Rosemarie, playing the role of the model father. But appearances deceive.

Two years later, Elisabeth started at Amstetten Middle School (Hauptschule), and soon after her eleventh birthday, she later told police, her father raped her for the first time.

The pre-pubescent girl was far too traumatized to tell anyone. From then on, she learned to endure his violent sexual attacks and live with her shocking secret. Today, more than thirty years later, she is still unable to talk about the circumstances of how he first raped her.

Whether his twisted obsession for his own daughter was rooted in the incestuous feelings he admits having for his mother remains a mystery. But over the next few years he began a sexual relationship with Elisabeth, taking her by force whenever he wanted.

Despite all the tension between father and daughter, and his mother imprisoned upstairs, Rosemarie Fritzl never appeared to notice there was anything untoward going on under her own roof.

Josef Fritzl had always been ambitious, working hard to better himself—a valuable lesson learned from his mother. He was now dabbling in property, buying and selling houses around Amstetten and Lower Austria. While his wife was conveniently far away, running the Mondsee Lake guest house and camping site, Josef spent summers in Amstetten, looking after the children.

In summer 1977, Rosemarie left for an Italian beach vacation, taking all her children except Elisabeth, who remained in Amstetten at her father's insistence.

Later she would tell police investigators how the rapes had escalated then, taking place in the cellar of their home, on the leather seats of his Mercedes or during walks through the forest.

"I don't know why it was so," she told police, "but my father simply chose me for himself."

"That is not true," Fritzl would say in May 2008. "I am not a man that has sex with little children. I only had sex with her later, much later," maintaining that he had controlled his unnatural urges, at least until Elisabeth was 18, just as he had claimed to have withheld his sexual impulses years earlier with his mother.

For years, Elisabeth would be too ashamed to tell anyone about his attacks, later confiding in several close friends.

Although Josef Fritzl was raping his daughter at will, he thought nothing of later sitting down across from her at the family dinner table, jovially cracking his favorite off-color jokes.

As she matured, he became increasingly possessive, insisting she come straight home from school and never talk to boys. One of her classmates would later recall Elisabeth's terror, if she was ever late getting home after school.

"When we went to her home," said the friend, "we had to leave as soon as her father appeared."

He would also violently punish her if she ever dared to wear makeup or dress in what he considered to be sexually provocative clothes.

Over time, her father's constant sexual abuse changed Elisabeth from a strong-willed, outgoing girl into a shy, nervous recluse.

"I remember that Elisabeth as a child was very withdrawn and shy," recalled Paul Hoerer, who visited the Fritzls' home several times over this period. "I got the impression [Josef] did not like her very much."

On one occasion, Hoerer even witnessed Josef Fritzl beating her for some minor infraction.

"He used to beat [Elisabeth] a lot more than the others," he recalled. "She used to get a slap for every small thing."

Hoerer also observed how his friend would change from being "a good laugh," when they were out dining, to "a bit of a dictator," when he got home.

"He could really get furious," he recounted, "and become another person."

But that was nothing compared to what Elisabeth endured on the days he demanded her body to satisfy his sexual cravings. He now regarded his little Liesel as his personal property—the ultimate expression of his own flesh and blood.

And like a proud collector of rare, exotic butterflies,

Fritzl dreamed of one day mounting his ultimate specimen in a glass case, where no one but him could enjoy her rare beauty.

In 1978, Josef Fritzl first conceived of building a dungeon in his cellar, to permanently imprison his then–12-year-old daughter Elisabeth, to be his personal sex slave. It would take him another six years to construct it to his obsessively demanding specifications.

Since his own 18-month jail sentence for rape a decade earlier, he had been searching for a woman to submit to his perverse sadistic desires. Although he was still regularly visiting prostitutes, many wanted nothing to do with him, because of his perverted demands. In his warped mind, he wanted to create his own personal kingdom where he reigned like a god.

It would be his personal re-creation of the Amstetten Mauer death camp he'd seen as a little boy, but for the time being it would only have one inmate—his beautiful daughter.

He started drawing up plans for his bunker, to be built around the original 1890 cellar of his large gray townhouse. Always practical, he decided to extend the back of his house at the same time, to construct eight small rental apartments for extra income.

He realized he could even have the Austrian state finance his sadistic enterprise by pretending to construct a domestic nuclear shelter, eligible for generous grants during the Cold War.

That summer, he submitted plans to the Amstetten planning authority for a basement extension, along with an application for a state grant.

But he secretly planned something far more ambitious—an elaborate windowless dungeon to imprison Elisabeth, and raise a secret family with her.

The house's long-forgotten original cellar would provide the nucleus, with several other rooms running off
it. There would be a ventilation pipe for air, as well as
an underground furnace for waste. A bathroom, kitchen
and toilet would be plumbed into the utility systems of
his main house. He would also wire the dungeon for
electricity, as well as soundproofing it so no one upstairs could hear anything.

His plans called for two separate entrances. One
would go directly from the cellar of his house, with no
fewer than eight locked doors, including three that
required electronic codes. The largest one, weighing
half a ton, would be hidden in a room beneath the stairs.
The second entrance would be accessible through a secret door at the end of his garden.

"From the very beginning he planned a prison,"
Austrian Police Chief Inspector Franz Polzer would
later relate. "He was obsessed [and] he went to elaborate lengths."

On October 31, 1978, the Amstetten town planning
department granted Josef Fritzl permission to build a
twenty-four-square-yard underground nuclear shelter—
just one-seventh the size of what he'd really had in
mind.

It would be a Herculean task. Over the next five
years he would single-handedly remove 250 tons of
earth from the ground, which would have taken seventeen trucks to carry away.

The brilliant engineer and technician would utilize
his skills in pouring reinforced concrete to line the
floors, walls and ceiling. He worked hard, with dedication and pride, as his wife and children lived upstairs,
blissfully unaware of his six-year-long secret mission.

During all the years of hard work, Josef Fritzl would

carefully file every single bill for materials and appliances, keeping a running total of his outlay. And he always shopped for bargains, delighting in getting the cheapest prices.

To ensure complete privacy, he planted evergreen trees and shrubbery bushes around his garden, creating a natural screen from his neighbors. Eventually, the back of his house would resemble a solid windowless concrete bunker, just like the ones he had seen as a child, built by the Nazis to resist heavy air attack.

"All the gardens are open while Herr Fritzl's is all concealed," said his neighbor Regina Penz, who lived three doors away. "You can't see anything."

Her husband Herbert remembers Fritzl laboring for years on his cellar, often hearing the sound of his cement mixer in his garden.

"[He] was always very hard-working," Penz recalled. "I think [he] did most of the work himself. We thought he was adding on an extra room to rent out, or something like that."

Gertrud Ramharter, who then lived directly across the street from Ybbsstrasse 40, remembers hammering and other loud construction sounds emanating from the Fritzl residence.

"What's he building?" she wondered. "And how big is it going to be?"

When Josef Fritzl eventually finished excavating his cellar, he secretly brought in vast quantities of bricks, tiles, wall panels and pipes. Much of the work was done during the summer when Rosemarie was running the guest house in Mondsee Lake, and she would proudly tell friends how hard he was working back in Amstetten.

"Rosemarie once told me, 'Josef is busy at home at the moment,'" remembered Elfriede Hoera. "'He has lots of building work to do.'"

Later there would be speculation that Fritzl must have had help excavating and building the cellar, but nothing has ever been proven.

"Fritzl appears to have done all this by himself," said Chief Inspector Polzer. "What this man did is beyond comprehension."

While secretly building her future prison downstairs, Josef Fritzl continued raping Elisabeth. As she blossomed into a beautiful teenager, he became obsessed that other boys in her class might be interested in her. The terrible pressures of being forced to submit to her father's twisted desires were now overwhelming her.

At Amstetten Middle School, she had become best friends with Christa Goetzinger and her twin sister Jutta, who sat two rows behind her. The 11-year-olds were all considered "outsiders," as their parents were not as affluent as those of the other girls in class. Although Josef Fritzl always dressed well, buying expensive Italian suits and silk ties, Elisabeth often arrived at school looking like a pauper.

"[The Fritzls] had very little money, and that meant that although [she] got fresh clothes on Monday, [she] was still wearing them on Friday," said Christa.

Elisabeth and the Goetzinger twins shared a tough home life and strict parents, but at the time Christa had no idea what her friend was going through. "We were always together," Christa remembered. "Elisabeth never talked about her father, except to say that he was very strict. I never really met him, but I saw her mother sometimes in school. She was very nice and polite, but not anything unusual."

For the next four years, Elisabeth and the twins were inseparable. They shared a love of music, especially

Schlager—a style of romantic folk music highly popular in Austria in the 1970s.

"Elisabeth loved music and sang in the school choir," Christa remembered. "We listened to various pop artists when we were kids. She loved ABBA and the Bee Gees, but she really loved Schlager."

Christa and Jutta came from a musical family, performing ABBA hits and Schlager songs at concerts after school and on weekends. But Elisabeth was never around to see them play.

"Her father would not allow her to go anywhere," said Christa. "She was a very quiet girl and never complained."

In hindsight, Christa remembers the change in her friend around the time that her father's sexual abuse began.

"Elisabeth became very sullen and withdrawn," she said. "She wasn't allowed out in the evenings or to invite her friends home. We laughed and talked about boys, [but] Elisabeth never did. I remember thinking at the time that was strange, and now I realize why."

After school, the three girls would often walk home together, occasionally buying candy from a local store if they had the money. Elisabeth particularly loved Brause sherbet powder.

"Elisabeth always had to be home at the latest half an hour after school had finished," said Christa. "Then she had to do her homework and study. We were always jealous of the other children, who were allowed out occasionally to go to the playground. We were forced to stay home."

It was obvious Elisabeth dreaded going home after school, and Christa would wonder why.

"She felt more comfortable at school than at home,"

Christa recalled. "Sometimes she went quiet when it was time to go home."

During the five years they were best friends, Elisabeth never once invited Christa back to her house on Ybbsstrasse.

"The only explanation she ever gave," said Christa, "was that her father was very strict. I never saw him, but he was always there between us—like an invisible presence."

CHAPTER 5

"The Pig Will Beat Us to Death One Day"

By the early 1980s, Josef Fritzl was approaching middle age. Although fully occupied building his dungeon, he still found time to drive to Linz, to visit the Villa Ostende brothel. While his family was struggling financially, Fritzl lived the good life, indulging in expensive Mediterranean holidays, champagne and hookers.

In Austria, prostitution is legal, and the Villa Ostende has a high turnover of girls, mostly coming from Eastern Europe. Since 1970, Fritzl had been a regular at the brothel, becoming notorious for his bizarre sexual demands, including having the $225-an-hour hookers play corpses, while he pleasured himself.

Many girls of the establishment were so creeped out by him, they refused his business—something extremely uncommon in Austrian brothels.

"He visited two or three times a week," Villa Ostende owner Peter Stolz, 60, later told the *News of the World*. "He always wanted all the works, but wanted to pay the least amount of money. And he had the most warped and perverted fantasies of anyone."

According to Stolz, the outwardly respectable businessman tortured his girls to the edge of death to achieve sexual gratification. He especially liked to tie up a prostitute, so she was helpless. Then he would furiously order her into a sack, tying the end shut until she was near suffocation, while berating her.

"I want to hear you gasping for breath," he'd scream. "I want to see you on the point of dying, [then] I will let you free again."

According to Stolz, Fritzl could only achieve orgasm by having the power over life and death.

"He had a God complex that was out of control," Stolz explained. "He was extremely perverse and needed to torture in order to be sexually satisfied."

On other occasions he indulged in violent rape fantasies. First he would have a girl put on heavy makeup with scarlet lipstick, before hunting her down and raping her.

"He insisted that the rape had to be real," said Stolz.

At other times he would have a prostitute savagely beat him up, until he achieved orgasm.

Villa Ostende barman Christoph Flugel described Josef Fritzl as *the* cheapest customer he had ever seen in all his years working there.

"If he would consume drinks for ninety-seven euros, and would pay with a hundred-euro bill," Flugel told the Austrian daily newspaper *Osterreich*, "he would demand the three euros back."

As he got to know Fritzl better, Flugel realized he was far more interested in dominance and humiliation than actual sex.

"He was bossy with everyone," Flugel remembered. "If he liked a girl, he would order champagne for her. But after a short while he would start behaving like a headmaster with pupils, saying things like, 'Sit straight!' or 'Don't speak nonsense!' Such behavior is unusual in sex clubs—you go there to relax and have fun."

Flugel said the girls would later discuss Fritzl's un-natural sexual demands, including some involving ex-crement or pretending to be a corpse.

"He got completely [off] track," Flugel said. "Per-verse. Two of them said, 'Never again with that guy.' Such a thing is very rare in this business."

Josef Fritzl compartmentalized his life, moving smoothly from one area to another without missing a beat. Apart from the increasing time and energy he devoted to satisfying his sexual needs, as well as con-structing his daughter's future prison, he was also start-ing to make money.

At the beginning of the 1980s, he began selling real estate and further dabbling in property development. He eventually bought five houses in Lower Austria, in-cluding a home less than two miles from Ybbsstrasse 40. He also later ran a short-lived mail-order lingerie business.

Fritzl was now projecting the image of a successful Amstetten businessman. He had shaved off his mus-tache and was buying expensive Italian suits to play his new role to perfection. He began frequenting bars and dance clubs in Amstetten such as the James Dean Club, although only drinking coffee with double milk, as he always had to be in control.

Back at home, he feared he was losing control of Elisabeth, as she grew into a beautiful young girl.

"She was so pretty, she could have had boyfriends," remembered Christa Goetzinger, "but she never did. She just sat quietly and no one noticed her. Unlike the other girls, she never talked about getting married or having children."

Another of Elisabeth's classmates later told the German magazine *Stern* how all the Fritzl children were terrified of their father.

"He didn't slap or spank them," said the friend, who wanted to remain anonymous. "He hit them with his fists. Her brother once told me, 'The pig will beat us to death one day.'"

Another of Elisabeth's brothers was so petrified of his father that whenever he heard his key turning in the front door lock, he would hide in a corner of the front room and wet his pants.

Elfriede Hoera once witnessed Josef Fritzl's violent abuse first-hand, when his daughter Rosemarie disobeyed him at the Mondsee Lake campground. She watched in horror as Fritzl dragged the sobbing little girl out of a caravan by her hair, slapping her hard across the face with his open hand.

"Josef was very cruel to them," said Hoera. "Rosemarie told me it was very common for him to attack them. They always burst into tears."

On another occasion, she saw him fly into a rage and attack several of his children outside Ybbsstrasse 40.

"Josef was driving down the road one night," she recalled, "and saw the kids running around. He stopped the car and got out in the middle of the street and started beating them. It was awful—I heard the screams."

Concerned for the children's welfare, Elfriede once asked Rosemarie why Josef appeared to love some of his children, but hated others. Rosemarie said she had no idea, noting that Ulrike was his favorite, as he respected her for daring to answer him back.

One day Rosemarie told Elfriede that she hated "the bastard" and was only happy when he was out of the house.

"My marriage is made up of quarrels and arguments," she tearfully told her friend. "We haven't had sex for a very long time, though I'm happy when he doesn't touch me."

Another of her friends, Roswita Zmug, called the Fritzls' marriage a complete sham.

"The marriage was over," she told London's *Sunday People* newspaper. "There was a coldness between them and they couldn't even talk to each other. Fritzl would just sit in the bar all day, ogling women and grinning, as if he had no cares in the world, while she ran around doing all the work."

Later many would ask why no one had ever reported Josef Fritzl to the police, after witnessing his physical abuse of his children. But in the 1960s and 1970s, it was common in Lower Austria for the patriarch to discipline his children.

According to *Stern* magazine, Josef Fritzl, in line with many fathers, used Scheitlknien, a traditional punishment dating back to the Austrian–Hungarian empire, which was then perfectly legal. Disobedient children were made to kneel for up to an hour on a sharply cut log of wood until they bled. In another punishment he poured rice seeds onto the marble-tiled kitchen floor, before making the unfortunate child stand on top of them in bare feet, arms outstretched horizontally, while balancing a heavy book.

Then, as they weakened and fell to the ground, Fritzl would whip them.

"Elisabeth learnt to take the beatings," said Christa Goetzinger, "to pull [herself] together when the pain was unendurable."

Christa and her twin sister Jutta said Elisabeth often excused herself from sports, ashamed that others would see the heavy bruising from her father's beatings.

"But she never spoke about what her father was doing to her," said Christa. "I never realized the truth about what was happening."

Christa believes that as her friend got older, she only ever felt "comfortable" in school, although she was not a particularly good student.

Alfred Dubanovsky, who was in Elisabeth's class at technical school, spent a lot of time with her.

"She was a great girl," said Dubanovsky, who would later rent a room in Josef Fritzl's house, "but very shy and pretty nervous. You needed to get to know her before she would trust you.

"We used to go to the Belami disco on her road, Ybbsstrasse, but she was rarely allowed to see us."

In summer 1981, 15-year-old Elisabeth Fritzl left Amstetten Technical School with average grades. On the last day of school, after getting her report card, she said good-bye to the Goetzinger twins, who were going off to Tyrol to study catering. Elisabeth complained that she wanted to be a cosmetician, but her father was insisting she work at his guest house restaurant.

In a school photograph taken shortly before she left, a fresh-faced Elisabeth is pictured with the twins, her classmates and teachers. The beautiful teenager, wearing a plain starched white blouse, stands out from the other girls with her enigmatic smile.

"I was very sad to say good-bye to Elisabeth, after we'd become so close," said Christa. "We promised to write to each other, but we lost contact. That would be the last time I would ever see her."

A few months later, Josef Fritzl used his business connections to find Elisabeth a job as a waitress at a local highway rest stop. For the next three years she learned the hospitality business while working at the busy Rosenberger diner at Strengberg, on the main A1 Autobahn, linking Vienna to Salzberg.

It was just thirteen miles away from Amstetten, and part of a chain of eleven motorway restaurants dotted throughout Austria. Fritzl reportedly thought it excellent training so she could prepare him meals when the dungeon was completed.

She was first sent on a two-month initiation course at a technical college in Waldegg, a small town 100 miles southeast of Amstetten. Reluctantly her father allowed her to share a dormitory below the kitchen with the other female students.

Elisabeth was overjoyed to finally get away from her father's clutches and his constant sexual demands. She felt liberated, praying he would let her finally start living her own life.

Over the two months she studied there, Elisabeth made several close friends, whom she confided in about her father's abuse.

"Sissy always wanted to run away," said a fellow trainee waitress. "She was always afraid of her father, and she told her friends about that."

After completing the initiation, Elisabeth moved back to the family home in Amstetten, where life continued as before. Each day she took the twenty-minute bus ride to the Strengberg Rosenberger restaurant, always putting on a cheerful face for her customers, however much turmoil she was going through inside.

Like the other rest stop staff, Elisabeth wore traditional Austrian dirndl dress, while serving coffee and snacks to customers on the busy Autobahn. She was popular with the other employees, occasionally going out after work with them to local bars and nightclubs.

"She was so quiet and nice to everyone," remembered Franz Hochwallner, who worked as a cook at the restaurant while Elisabeth was there.

None of them dreamed of the unspeakable horrors that awaited her most nights after she got the bus home.

The year 1982 marked the fifteenth anniversary of Josef Fritzl's rape conviction. It was officially expunged, in accordance with the strict Austrian privacy law, leaving him with a clean record.

A few months later he was arrested again and charged with arson after another suspicious fire at his Mondsee Lake guest house. At the police station, he was photographed clean-shaven before being booked. But after spending a short time in Unterach prison, he was released because of lack of any evidence against him.

"Everyone thought he set fire to the place," recalled Beate Schmidinger, who owned a café nearby, "because we knew he had money trouble."

In any case, from now on, at least in the eyes of the Austrian authorities, Josef Fritzl was a citizen beyond reproach, with a clean slate. It was as if he had never crawled in through the window that 1967 night in Linz, savagely raping a young nurse at knifepoint. Now, under the Austrian legal system, he would enjoy the same privileges as any other upright citizen.

CHAPTER 6

Escape

On January 28, 1983, Elisabeth Fritzl and another Rosenberger waitress went out to a bar, after finishing their shifts. After a few drinks, Elisabeth broke down in tears, telling how her father had been raping her since she was 11. Describing her home life as "hell," she said she had to get out.

That night, the two 17-year-olds decided to run away together.

"I knew Sissy was being raped by her father," said Josef Leitner, an Amstetten waiter who had known Elisabeth at Amstetten Technical College, and would later become one of her father's tenants. "I had a good friend from school who was really close to her. She told me what a monster Josef was and what he had done to Sissy. She could not take it to live at home anymore, and tried to escape . . . she packed her bags and left."

According to Leitner, Elisabeth and their mutual friend, whose identity he would not reveal, spent several days in Linz before going to Vienna, a big city where there would be less chance of them being caught. They found a cheap apartment in the Hartlgasse 42 district, and went into hiding.

When Josef Fritzl learned she had run away, he was

livid, and reported her missing, prompting an Interpol hunt. He also dispatched his son Harald—who was close to Elisabeth—to search for her in the Vienna red-light district. He was petrified that Elisabeth was free, and might now betray him as a sexual predator.

Eventually, after three weeks on the run, police picked up the teenage girls at a Vienna party, after neighbors complained about the noise. They were taken to a police station, where Josef Fritzl collected his daughter the next morning and drove her home.

"Josef was furious," said Leitner. "Sissy was banned from having anything to do with my friend again. Her mother also made sure of that. She watched her carefully to make sure they were kept apart."

From then on, Josef Fritzl would always describe his daughter as his black sheep, an unruly troubled child with alcohol and substance abuse problems.

By running away, Elisabeth had unwittingly provided him with the ammunition he would later need to explain her sudden disappearance, when he was finally ready to bring her down into the dungeon.

For the first few weeks after her return, Josef Fritzl didn't touch his teenage daughter, but eventually he couldn't control himself.

Later, she would tell police how she had decided to stick it out, submitting to his sexual demands for the time being. There was only another eighteen months left in her hospitality training program, she reasoned. Then she would be free to leave home and become a chef, never having to see her father again.

That summer, Elisabeth spent a few weeks working as a waitress in a Tyrolean motel in Angath, 185 miles west of Amstetten. A photograph taken at the motel shows the pretty 17-year-old, wearing a red-and-white traditional Austrian dirndl dress, looking like she'd come straight out of *The Sound of Music*.

But her colleagues remember her as being a troubled girl, with an alcohol problem.

"Sissy was the wildest party girl I have ever met," a fellow worker named Heidi would later tell *News of the World*. "She was always sneaking out the window of our dorm at night to meet up with boys. And then she would stay out all night drinking, dancing and having fun."

According to Heidi, Elisabeth often stayed out all night, turning up the following morning unfit to work.

"She partied hard and worked as little as she could," she said. "She could down more beer, schnapps and wine than most."

Eventually her boss threatened to fire her and send her back to Amstetten if she didn't calm down.

"I'll never forget the sudden change in her," said Heidi. "She burst into tears. She told me, 'If they really send me home, I will run away immediately, because I cannot stand being at home anymore.'"

After that, she stopped drinking, completing her assignment in Angath before returning to Amstetten and her old job at the Rosenberger restaurant.

By the fall of 1983, Josef Fritzl was putting the finishing touches to his dungeon, now six years in the making. The ever-resourceful 48-year-old engineer had single-handedly created an engineering marvel of unparalleled evil.

He had recently rented an industrial winch, attaching it to the roof of his three-story house. It was positioned directly over the cellar to hoist massive concrete blocks into place, turning his bunker into an impenetrable fortress.

After devising a crude ventilation system to pump oxygen into the network of rooms, he brought in a fridge, gas cooker and toilet, so the dungeon would be self-sufficient. He also wired it for electricity, installed a gas furnace to burn rubbish and lined the walls and ceilings with cork and other soundproofing materials, ensuring that no one upstairs could hear anything down below.

Always thrifty, Fritzl kept a careful watch on every cent he spent on his dark obsession, buying second-hand wherever possible. He was intensely proud of his creation, and would later describe in detail how he had constructed it.

"I got a really heavy concrete-and-steel door," he recounted, "that worked with an electric motor and a remote control that I used to get into the cellar. It needed a number code to open and close.

"I then plastered the walls, added something to wash in and a small toilet, a bed and a cooking ring, as well as a fridge, electricity and lights."

Over the entire six years it took him to complete the dungeon, not one of his neighbors, tenants or anybody else ever questioned what he was doing.

"Perhaps some people did notice," he said later. "But they really did not care—why should they? At the end of the day, the cellar of my house belongs to me. It is my kingdom only I can enter. That is what everyone knew who lived in the area. That includes my wife, my children and my tenants. And none of them ever managed to force their way into my kingdom, or asked me what I did there."

When he was finally ready to have it officially inspected by the Amstetten planning authority, he cemented all entries closed, concealing the full extent of his excavations. He had also managed to dig a passage through to the original 1890 cellar under the main house, which he would eventually use to enlarge the dungeon.

On July 26, 1983, a team of planning inspectors visited his cellar. Finding nothing untoward, they rubber-stamped their approval for his "nuclear shelter," signing off on a generous state grant toward its construction.

But it would be another year of final preparations before the always-patient Josef Fritzl would finally trick his daughter Elisabeth into going down there.

On April 16, 1984, Elisabeth Fritzl celebrated her 18th birthday, and was full of hope for the future. She had almost completed her three-year catering course, enthusiastically making plans to move in with her sister Ulrike, and finally get away from her father forever.

Over the last few months, he had somewhat relaxed his domination over her, and Elizabeth had spent time in an apartment away from home. She had a new set of friends, and was especially proud of her new fashionable pageboy haircut. She had started going out to discos and bars at night, and had started drinking again.

She also had a steady boyfriend she had met at a catering course, and was heartbroken when he moved to another town to continue his studies. Outwardly she was just like any other teenage girl, but inside she still bore the open scars of her father's seven years of savage sexual abuse.

On May 9—a few weeks before she was due to take her final catering exams—Elisabeth wrote to an old friend and former student named Ernst. Apparently, she had confided in him about her father's abuse, and was replying to a "nice long" letter he had recently sent her.

Basically, I'm doing pretty fine. Sometimes I get pains and I feel sick again. I'm supposed to be off sick at the moment, but I am completely stressed out. My nerves are not in good shape either.

Then she went on to discuss some old friends from a course they had both attended, including the one she was having a difficult long-distance relationship with.

I'm only in contact with [name withheld] still. He went into the next hospitality class for cooks and waiters. I've been dating him since the course. Sometimes there are problems because he is from Enzesfeld-Lindabrunn. This is very far from my place and this is why I am very sad.

She then asked Ernst to keep his "fingers crossed," as she was applying for a job outside Amstetten.

After the exams, I'm moving in with my sister and her boyfriend. As soon as I've moved I will send you my new address . . . You could come and visit me with your friends if you want to.
I had my hair cut . . . layered on the sides and on the fringe. At the back I want to let it grow long.

She then asked Ernst about his home life, and how tolerant his parents were.
"Do you have parties when your parents are at home, too?" she wanted to know.

You are a crazy guy. I have a sensitive question I want to ask. I'd like to know if we're going to stay friends when you have a girlfriend? Most of the time friendships break up because of that, and it is very important to me.

Then Elisabeth discussed her close relationship with her brother Harald, who had been sent to bring her back from Vienna a year earlier.

If you can believe it, I deal with boys better than girls. Girls are not as trustworthy as boys. Probably that's because I was around my brother from when I was a little child. I am very proud of my brother, who is now 21 years old. I know his problems and he knows mine, and I wouldn't say anything bad about him.

Three weeks later, Elisabeth wrote another letter to Ernst on notepaper, decorated with a dancing girl in a yellow dress. She was still recovering after a late night of drinking with her "crew," but expressing optimism for the future.

"Hello Ernst," she began.

It is now already half-past-ten and I'm lying in bed. Of course I went out Saturday. Can you imagine how hammered I was? At first we went to a couple of clubs. At about 5:00 A.M. we all went to my place to get a coffee, because we'd had so much fun. They are really cool. And they all slept at my place. That was a mess. It took me half-a-day to clean up the flat.

Then she wrote about her job, saying she looked forward to her upcoming two days off.

That's when I go swimming, play tennis or even football. I like listening to music and daydreaming. But if life consists just of dreams, well I don't really know about that.

Then she signed the letter "S," telling Ernst,

Stay safe, keep being a good boy. Don't drink too much.

Waiting patiently in the wings, Josef Fritzl was well aware of his daughter's new set of friends and her drinking. And although he hated her going out and having a good time with boys, he cunningly knew that the reputation she was now getting in Amstetten as a wild girl would prove very useful.

He had now almost finished the dungeon, and his final task was to winch the huge sliding three-foot-by-two-foot steel door frame into the cellar. He then sprayed it with liquid concrete. When it dried, it would weigh 660 pounds, and seal off his prison from the outside world.

Now everything was in place, and he was ready to make his move.

CHAPTER 7

Brief Encounter

In early June, Elizabeth went to Waldegg on a two-month catering course. She would take her final exams at the end of the intensive training program, and already had an offer of a good waitress job in Linz, if she got good grades.

An 18-year-old student cook named Andreas Kruzik, was immediately attracted to the beautiful young girl, striking up a conversation with her.

"I saw her in the school yard for the first time," he remembered. "[She was] a pretty girl, but serious and withdrawn."

Over the first weeks of the course they became a couple, soon falling in love. And the more time they spent together, the more relaxed Elisabeth became in his company.

"I noticed that she was slowly opening up," he said, "and started to show an interest in me."

At the school the sexes were strictly segregated, and any male student caught in a female dormitory would be expelled immediately.

"We were a couple," he said. "But it was not so simple to be intimate, because such things were not allowed in the school. And there were only a few opportunities to make out."

Eventually the couple found a quiet place in the forest where they would not be disturbed. They would sneak off together, spending hours kissing and talking about their lives.

"We could be close and gentle to each other," said Andreas. "She was very tender, but also very timid."

After all the years of violent sexual attacks from her father, Elisabeth could not bring herself to have sex, pulling back at the last moment.

"We never slept with each other," he recalled. "She did not want to—or was not able to."

They also took day trips to Vienna, on one memorable occasion seeing the hit Broadway musical *West Side Story.*

During their month together, Elisabeth sometimes spoke of her family and her miserable home life.

"She really confided in me," said Andreas. "I knew that she was under pressure from her parents, and that she ran away from home when she was fourteen or fifteen. She was closer to some of her siblings than others, and there was a trusted sister who she stayed with often."

One time, she spoke of her father and his controlling ways, without mentioning his sexual abuse.

"[She] said she had a very strict father," he recalled. "He had got her a waitress apprenticeship at a tank station, but she would have preferred to have been a cosmetician."

As the course came to an end, they discussed running away together and starting a new life.

"We talked about the future and getting married," he explained. "We were madly in love."

On the final night, they attended a student party, celebrating the end of exams. Elisabeth had just learned she had failed an important one, and was inconsolable.

She feared it might jeopardize the Linz job, and her dreams of escaping Amstetten forever.

"Sissy had too much wine to drink and became all hyper," Andreas recalled. "She was very depressed and worried. She had failed part of an exam—the theory part. But I was cracking jokes and trying to cheer her up. I said, 'Don't worry, you can repeat the exams.'"

"That night she said she wanted to sleep with me after the party," he said, "and planned to stay at [my place]," after the students went home the next day.

But early the next morning, Josef and Rosemarie arrived unexpectedly, to bring their daughter back to Amstetten. Elisabeth sadly told her boyfriend she would have to go with them, promising to stay in touch through letters, until they could be together again.

"I wasn't allowed to see her out," he said, "because her father was not supposed to see me, and she would have been in trouble if he did. I kissed her good-bye and said I would be down to Amstetten to visit her. But she was worried about her dad. He was outside waiting in the car, and she feared that if he found out about me, she would be punished."

Then Andreas sadly watched from a dormitory window, as Elisabeth climbed into Josef Fritzl's gleaming gray Mercedes-Benz and disappeared down the drive. It would be the last time he would ever see her.

A week later, on August 3, Elisabeth wrote her final letter to her friend Ernst, while watching the 1971 Steven Spielberg movie thriller *Duel* on television. She informed him she would soon be moving in with her elder sister Ulrike, but was completely stressed out by exams, writing:

Cross your fingers for me. When you get this letter, it will all be over. I'll give you my new address as soon as I've moved.

She also told of going to a local fair with workmates, saying, "that was something."

Now I'm very tired because it's very late. And also the evening movie is so exciting. I can't write while watching this.
    Bye, see you soon,
    S.
Write back soon and don't get drunk for no reason.

She attached a new color Polaroid of herself, sitting on the steps of her parents' rooftop pool, wearing a flowery blouse and jeans, and sporting a smart new bobbed haircut.

On the back she wrote:

PS, the picture is a bit dark, but I will send you better ones soon, OK?
    Think of me,
    Sissy.

After their emotional parting, Andreas Kruzik wrote Elisabeth two passionate love letters, mailing them to her family home at Ybbsstrasse 40. He mentioned their plans to elope and settle down together, telling her he was more in love with her than ever. He also wrote of their future life together after they married and had children.

But Elisabeth never read them, as her father got there

first. After reading them, he became incandescent with rage, and jealous of their love affair.

He had already noticed that since returning from the course, she seemed to have a new sense of independence. Now he knew why. He was furious at the thought of another man touching her body—his flesh and blood. He realized he was finally losing control over her, something he could never allow to happen.

Now the time had come to initiate his plan, and lure his daughter into the dungeon, so she could be his forever.

By mid-August, Elisabeth was worried when she had heard nothing from Andreas, although he had promised to write. Since her return to Amstetten, her father had been more brutal than ever, viciously beating her on several occasions.

He now refused to allow her to leave the house, apart from working her shifts at the Rosenberger restaurant, and he no longer let her go to the Belami disco for her regular evening out with friends.

She had made up her mind to run away again.

"[Sissy] had told someone in our group that she had had enough," said her old Amstetten school friend Alfred Dubanovsky, "and couldn't stand it anymore at home, and that her father had beat her, and had hurt her. She said she was scared of him."

CHAPTER 8

Taken

Tuesday, August 28, 1984, was a beautiful late summer day in Amstetten. Golden rays of sun streamed into Elisabeth Fritzl's bedroom that morning, as she prepared for her shift at the Rosenberger restaurant.

A little before 9:00 a.m., her father walked into her room, asking if she would help him move a heavy steel door downstairs into the basement. She agreed.

She dutifully followed him down three flights of stairs to his workroom, which led to the cellar. When they reached the entrance, he asked her to help him drag the 600-pound steel-and-concrete door into position to seal it off.

Then suddenly, without warning, he pushed her into the cellar, grabbing the back of her head with one hand, and using his other to smother her face with an ether-soaked handkerchief.

Elisabeth desperately tried to fight him off, but she was no match for her powerful father. When she lost consciousness and dropped to the floor, he handcuffed her. He then dragged her through a long corridor with seven doors, and into his dungeon, throwing her onto a bed in the middle of the floor.

"He pushed me into this little room," she later told police. "Tied me up and somehow kept me quiet."

Like an animal he raped her again and again, until he was spent. Then he turned off the electric light, leaving her dazed in the pitch-black darkness, and left, carefully locking the eight heavy doors connecting the dungeon to the outside world.

Ironically, that day marked the forty-sixth anniversary of the opening of the Mauthausen concentration camps in Austria. It would be another 8,516 days before Elisabeth Fritzl would see daylight again.

Later, Elisabeth would remember waking up alone in the dark, finding herself handcuffed to a metal pole. As she slowly came out of her drugged state, the terrible truth dawned that she had been imprisoned by her father.

Time meant little in the dungeon. She had no way of knowing how long it was before she heard the door open, and her father appeared. He turned on the light and threw her back on the bed, repeatedly raping her like a wild animal. The terrified girl screamed as loudly as she could, but no one could hear.

"What followed was unimaginable brutality and sadism," said a detective, who later interviewed Elisabeth. "He raped, drugged and tortured his daughter, before leaving her manacled to the wall."

After he had gone, leaving her a bowl of food, she screamed until she was hoarse, banging on the walls as hard as she could. But he had soundproofed the dungeon so well, no one upstairs heard her desperate cries for help.

Two days later, he returned with more food and to rape her again. Once again she tried to fight him off, but he beat her mercilessly with his fists, until she gave up and stopped resisting.

Then after satisfying his twisted hunger, he tied an electric cable leash around her waist. It was just two yards long, allowing her to reach a small makeshift toilet he'd installed in one corner of her 15'9 × 15' prison. He attached another chain around her stomach.

"The only thing I could do was go to the toilet," she told police.

Over the next nine months he would slowly wear down Elisabeth until she gave up, resigning herself to her terrible fate of being his sex slave.

The first night Elisabeth didn't come home, her mother became very worried. Josef Fritzl seemed unusually sympathetic, staying up with Rosemarie and trying to console her, saying the girl had probably run away again.

And the next day, when their daughter had still not appeared, Josef and Rosemarie Fritzl went to Amstetten police station to report her missing. Her anxious father told police how she had run away in the past, and had probably done so again.

"From one day to the next she just vanished," a police report at the time quoted Rosemarie as saying.

Over the next few days Josef Fritzl went through the motions of searching for his daughter. He and Rosemarie turned up at the Rosenberger restaurant, concerned for Elisabeth's safety. Fritzl told her boss, Franz Perner, that she had run away, asking if any of the other waitresses might know where she had gone. No one did.

Over the next few days, Josef Fritzl continued his elaborate charade, fooling everyone. He and Rosemarie searched train stations, homeless shelters and bars, as he repeatedly berated their ungrateful daughter for causing them so much worry.

Rosemarie Fritzl was so heartbroken, she even consulted a fortune-teller, who shed little light on Elisabeth's disappearance.

For the first few terrifying weeks of her captivity, Josef Fritzl kept Elisabeth in the dark, humid dungeon with its low ceiling. His crudely designed ventilation system provided barely enough oxygen, making her tired and lethargic.

Several times a day he would come to rape her, before giving her scraps of food. Later she would tell police that she had no choice but to submit to his violent sexual attacks or starve to death.

Her thoughts during those interminable hours of waiting for his next visit, while tethered to the pole in the dark, only she will ever know. Day and night no longer existed in this hell, and she could not even chalk off the hours, days and weeks, like a prisoner in solitary confinement.

Later she would tell police how she "quaked with fear" each time she heard the sound of the electronic sliding door opening, knowing her tormentor had arrived to satisfy his twisted sexual hunger.

At first she tried to fight back, but he beat her black and blue if she dared struggle. Then, after he'd left, she'd spend hours screaming and banging on the wall as hard as she could, but no one would ever come and rescue her.

It was all about control for Josef Fritzl, and this was the most enjoyable part of his game. It was a challenge to break his daughter's spirit with rape, torture and force—just like breaking in a wild horse and putting on a saddle.

When Andreas Kruzik didn't receive any reply to his letters from Elisabeth, he became more and more frustrated. He had thought they were a couple, and he could not fathom why she had suddenly broken off all contact.

He finally telephoned her Amstetten home. Her father answered, saying Elisabeth was unavailable and not to call back.

"I was palmed off," Andreas recalled. "It was over and I didn't hear from her again. I thought she had lost interest in me."

By mid-September, Elisabeth Fritzl had stopped fighting back, resigning herself to captivity, much in the way that Nazi death camp prisoners had once done. At this point Fritzl stopped beating her, although still forcing her to have sex with him.

One day her father came into the dungeon, and, after satisfying himself, produced a pen and paper to dictate a letter for her to write.

Dated September 21, 1984, the letter to her parents explained that she had gone off with a friend to join a religious cult, saying she didn't want to live at home any longer.

"Don't look for me," it said, asking them to respect her decision to live her own life, otherwise she would leave Austria forever. Then Fritzl made her address an envelope to him at Ybbsstrasse 40, Amstetten.

It must have been agonizing for Elisabeth to know that the letter would now cut off any possible chance of her being found.

Later that day, Josef Fritzl drove one hundred miles west to Braunau am Inn—where Adolf Hitler had been born almost a century earlier—and mailed it from a post office, so it bore a postmark from there. It would be the first of many cunning red herrings he would employ over the years to convince the world that Elisabeth had joined a mysterious cult.

Several days later, when the letter arrived at Ybbs-sstrasse 40, Rosemarie Fritzl read it with her husband. She was relieved that her daughter had been in touch, thinking that at least she was safe.

Josef Fritzl then brought the letter to Amstetten police, saying he had been right all along, and Elisabeth had run away. He then filled out an official missing persons report for his daughter.

Now confident that he had fooled everyone, he walked into the offices of a local newspaper, asking the editor to run a story about his daughter's disappearance, even supplying her photo for publication.

After an initial investigation, Amstetten police forwarded Elisabeth Fritzl's missing persons report to the Austrian Interior Ministry. Copies were also sent to the state financial authority and state education authorities. Interpol was also briefly brought in, but after questioning a number of religious sects, it came up with nothing.

Cunning Josef Fritzl's letter had paid off, and there never was a major police search, as he had so successfully cast Elisabeth in the role of a selfish runaway.

Police never stopped to consider what could possibly make a girl with good prospects, who was looking forward to a new job, run away, not once, but several times.

Now armed with the letter, Josef Fritzl began telling friends and neighbors that his wayward daughter had left home to join a sect.

"One day he came to my door and told me Elisabeth was not coming home anymore," remembered Anton Graf, who had rented him land at Mondsee Lake. "That she had left to join a cult."

Graf found Fritzl so convincing, he felt terrible for all the "suffering" Elisabeth had caused her family.

"He told us that a letter had arrived [which] said it was pointless to search for her, because she was deeply involved with the sect. She was happy there and she was definitely not coming home."

When he told his neighbor Regina Penz, she was not surprised.

"Elisabeth had already caused trouble before," she later told an English documentary team. "She had disappeared once before and then turned up again."

Regina said that if you had seven children, like the Fritzls, one of them was bound to be troublesome.

"You just accept [that] these things happen," she said. "It doesn't mean you've done anything wrong as a parent."

Another friend, Leopold Styetz, deputy mayor of the Upper Austrian town of Lasberg, vacationed with the Fritzls during that period. He liked Josef, respecting him as "an intelligent and successful businessman."

"He always liked to talk about his perfect family," Styetz recalled in 2008, "but he was very hard on his children. Whenever we asked him about Liesel, he used to say Interpol was looking for her. He said he was so worried that he even went to a fortune-teller, to try and learn what had happened to her."

When Elisabeth Fritzl's friends heard she had run away and joined a religious cult, they had mixed feelings. Alfred Dubanovsky was not suspicious, knowing she had recently discussed leaving home.

"After she vanished, we were talking about it," he remembered. "We knew she had run off before and we thought she had run off again, because she had told someone in our group she had had enough."

Another friend, Josef Leitner, wondered why police had never questioned any of her friends to find out why she might have run away.

"She ran away on more than one occasion," he said. "I'm surprised authorities didn't investigate more intensely. Why didn't they try and find out why Elisabeth wanted to run away again and again?"

Leitner now claims that many friends Elisabeth had confided in about her father's abuse were too scared of him to go to the police.

The waitress Elisabeth had earlier run away to Vienna with believed she had now gone to Amsterdam and become involved in drugs and prostitution.

Elisabeth's old school friend Christa Goetzinger says that although there was much gossip among their friends about Elisabeth joining a cult, she had never believed it.

"She was just not that type," she said. "Not Sissy."

CHAPTER 9

His Second Wife

In the weeks following Elisabeth's disappearance, Josef Fritzl painstakingly created what investigators would later describe as "a perfectly constructed framework of lies." He made numerous visits to Amstetten police station, angrily complaining that investigators were not doing enough to track down his runaway daughter. Over the next few years, he and his wife would give countless emotional interviews on television and in newspapers, as the devastated parents of a missing teenage girl.

"We spoke about it often when we met," remembered Christine. "And I would say, 'Rosemarie, where can Elisabeth be?' I even told myself she is definitely in a cult."

The two sisters even did their own investigation into which cult she had joined.

"We really did detective work," said Christine, "as to where the cult could be. But where can you find out where these cults are?"

Rosemarie Fritzl and her other children resumed their lives at Ybbsstrasse 40, unaware that three floors below, Elisabeth was living like a caged animal in the dank, airless dungeon. Her torturous existence was only punctuated by her father's visits for sex every two or three days.

Slowly she was forced to accept the bizarre new role he had planned for so long—his second wife, and the mother of a new subterranean family.

On April 16, 1985, Elisabeth turned 19 and the official search for her was called off, as, under Austrian law, she was no longer a minor and could go wherever she wanted. To celebrate, her father removed the cable leash from her waist, so she could walk around the tiny dungeon. Over the next few months, Elisabeth's relationship to her captor changed as her survival instincts kicked in.

"Since she was taken prisoner at the age of eighteen," said Professor Max Friedrich, the head of the Medical University of Vienna's Clinic for Child and Adolescent Psychiatry. "The question is, how did she cope with her fear, and at what point was her will broken?"

Professor Friedrich believes Elisabeth Fritzl is a textbook victim of Stockholm syndrome—a psychological condition where a hostage becomes sympathetic or loyal to their captors to survive. The syndrome was first identified in 1973, when a team of bank robbers took employees at the Kreditbanken in Stockholm, Sweden, hostage for six days. During that time the victims became emotionally attached to their captors, eventually resisting rescue attempts by the police, later refusing to even testify against the robbers. Two of the hostages eventually became engaged to their captors.

The term was first used in a media interview by Swedish psychiatrist Nils Bejerot, who had advised police during the incident.

A year later, American newspaper heiress Patty

Hearst went even further, after being kidnapped by the radical Symbionese Liberation Army. She eventually joined the group, participating in several bank robberies, and subsequently serving a 2-year jail sentence, later commuted by President Jimmy Carter.

"Psychologically," said renowned forensic psychiatrist and bestselling author Keith Ablow, M.D., "you would expect a constriction of [Elisabeth's] emotional world . . . to survive in circumstances like that. You need to deny a lot of suffering to focus on practical matters, like food and survival. You may well feel allied with your captor in a Stockholm way.

"The general paradigm would be a psyche twisting itself into the grotesque pattern of daily existence and normalizing it, in order to not go insane. And at a certain point you imagine hope being extinguished."

Dr. Ablow compares Elisabeth's psychological situation to anticipatory avoidance experiments with laboratory mice, where food would be placed on an electrified side of a cage. After repeatedly being shocked, the mice stop trying to retrieve the food, even after the electric current is turned off.

"And at a certain point," said Dr. Ablow, "the human mind shuts down too. 'I'll take my gains where they come. I didn't get beaten as much today. I got food today. It was a good day, underground here.'"

Kidnapped hostages, fearing for their lives, often start identifying with their captors as a psychological defense mechanism. Then even the smallest act of kindness is magnified, as there is little perspective in such a situation.

Always the master manipulator, Josef Fritzl exploited this, by softening his domination. He now began arriving with clothes and blankets and other small presents, in some kind of bizarre courting ritual. He was no longer as violent during sex, and stopped using any contraception, appearing to want to get his daughter pregnant.

In 2008, Fritzl would vehemently deny having any sexual relations with Elisabeth prior to that spring. Perhaps his denial revealed how his obsession had changed course, with him now viewing her as a beautiful new wife, instead of an unruly daughter.

Despite all the evidence to the contrary, he would claim they'd first had sex in spring 1985, as he could no longer control himself.

"The pressure to do the forbidden thing was just too big to withstand," he would explain. "At some stage somewhere in the night, I went into the cellar and laid her down on the bed and had sex with her."

He said she did not resist his advances by "scratching, biting or beating," just making "small whimpering noises," as he had his way.

Then after he'd finished raping her, he'd sit and chat as she hungrily ate her food. He would tell her news about her brothers and sisters, and how they were doing at school, as well as gossiping about life upstairs, what he had planted in his garden, or movies he had seen on television. And he'd tell her how upset her mother was since she had gone.

On the way out, he would always start tinkering with a gadget by the sliding steel door, warning her it was booby-trapped, and if she ever tried to escape, deadly gas would be automatically released into the dungeon.

Upstairs at Ybbsstrasse 40, Josef Fritzl ordered his family never to go into the cellar, saying it was his own private office with all his business files. His tenants were also banned from using his garden, keeping pets, or ever going into the backyard, with the threat of immediate eviction.

Before he allowed a prospective tenant to rent one of his eight rooms, he would warn that the cellar was out-of-bounds, and never to go anywhere near it. He also stressed that no photographs could be taken of it, and he would only allow them to move in after agreeing to his terms.

Any music or loud noises after 10:00 p.m., were also banned, on pain of eviction. Ironically, over the years, many tenants would hear mysterious sounds coming from the cellar. But they were far too scared of their landlord to ever investigate or complain.

Fritzl found tenants by placing ads in the local newspaper, always preferring ones on social security, guaranteeing a monthly government rent check.

In 1990, Josef Leitner, who now worked as a waiter, moved into Ybbsstrasse 40, even though he had once been told by a friend that his new landlord had raped his own daughter.

"She told me what a monster Josef was," recalled Leitner, who had studied with Elisabeth at a technical college before she disappeared. "But I did not want to get involved. I did not want to get kicked out of the room. I kept myself to myself."

Fritzl's overbearing attitude and tough set of rules led to a revolving door of tenants, with more than one hundred moving in and out over the years.

Soon after imprisoning Elisabeth, Josef Fritzl developed a regular routine, often spending entire nights in the cellar, telling Rosemarie he was busy on a new project that would make their fortune.

"Every day at nine o'clock he would go down in the

cellar," remembered his sister-in-law Christine, "supposedly to develop plans for machines that he would sell to businesses. Often he would spend whole nights down there. Rosi wasn't even allowed to bring him a coffee."

And no one in the family ever dared ask why he was now spending so much time down in the cellar.

"His word was law," explained Christine.

After Elisabeth's disappearance, her mother sank into a depression and began gaining more weight, causing her husband to humiliate her in public. It was common knowledge amongst their friends and family that they never had sex.

"He always put Rosi down and called her fat," recalled her sister. "[He said] 'chubby women are below my standard.'"

In September 1986, Elisabeth became pregnant with her father's child and fell into a deep depression. And when she miscarried alone at ten weeks, she contemplated suicide.

Her father showed no sympathy whatsoever, as he coldly disposed of the fetus, turning the lights off in the dungeon to punish her.

On November 12, 1986, two skin-divers found the bound body of 17-year-old Martina Posch on the shores of Lake Mondsee, near Josef Fritzl's boarding house. Later a friend would claim Fritzl had been staying there the day she disappeared.

The young girl, who closely resembled Elisabeth, had disappeared ten days earlier. Police said she had been raped and then wrapped in two green plastic covers, before being dumped by the picturesque lake. Her clothes and personal belongings have never been found.

It would be another twenty-two years before Austrian police would begin investigating Josef Fritzl for her murder.

By now, Josef Fritzl had become a pillar of the Amstetten community, considered a successful businessman, an upright citizen and a good family man. He dressed well, favoring expensive blazers, silk cravats and Italian patent leather shoes. Now in his early fifties and starting to lose his hair, he secretly went to Vienna for an expensive hair transplant.

"He is a very vain man," remembered his friend Gerda Schmidt. "His shoes were always glistening, his tie was never askew, he could have been a diplomat."

And he would often talk about how Elisabeth had run away to join a cult, and broken his and his wife's hearts.

"He often talked about his family," his friend Leopold Styetz told the London *Times*. "He was very strict with his children, a strict but fair father, I would say. It was enough for him to snap his fingers and the youngsters would be in bed already. He always stressed that, for him, education and career were *the* most important things."

By 1987, Josef Fritzl left with a friend for the first of several lengthy trips to Pattaya, the notorious Thailand sex resort. Before leaving, he packed the cellar's refrigerator with frozen food so his prisoner could feed herself while he was away. But she knew that if anything happened to him 5,000 miles away in Thailand, she would be doomed.

Later he would claim to have installed a mechanism to open the doors to the cellar and free his prisoner after a certain period of time. But that was a lie.

During his vacation, Fritzl played tourist during the day, riding elephants and sunbathing. His habit of using his beach towel to reserve sun loungers upset the other tourists at his hotel.

"Fritzl would lord it around us at the beach," recalled Briton Stephen Crickson, who was vacationing there with his girlfriend. "He treated staff with contempt. He was universally unpopular."

Later, Crickson would tell the London *Sun* how he'd once seen Fritzl walking hand in hand with a 16-year-old rent boy on the beach. And there was much gossip regarding the Austrian's nightly visits to the town's infamous "Boys Town" red-light area.

"He was a disgusting pervert," said Crickson, "and all the ex-pats and regular holidaymakers knew what he was up to. Rent boys, ladyboys, he would go with anything."

CHAPTER 10

Children of the Cellar

In 1988, four years after her father lured her into the basement, Elisabeth Fritzl became pregnant again. Now 22, she was terrified of her father's reaction, waiting as long as possible before informing him. But if she thought this would force him to set her free to go to a hospital for an abortion, she was sadly mistaken.

"Do not think you are getting away from me so easily," he told her, bringing in medical books to help her cope with her condition alone.

During the long months of her pregnancy, Elisabeth must have agonized over whether the incestuous baby would be healthy. From then on her relationship with Fritzl subtly changed from one of jailor and prisoner to husband and wife.

"If we want to discuss when things deteriorated for Elisabeth," said Professor Friedrich, "then certainly there was the moment when she realized that she was pregnant for the first time."

The professor says that at this point in her captivity, Josef Fritzl became less violent.

"There was a change," he explained. "She said herself that even before she was incarcerated, she'd been abused by her father. After being taken prisoner, [she] had endured brutal physical violence in some shape or form. And then she told us that this had lessened."

When his daughter became too visibly pregnant with his child, Fritzl stopped demanding sex, apparently no longer attracted to her. Then he abandoned her altogether, leaving her alone to deliver her baby in the unhygienic dungeon.

Later Fritzl would give his version of his daughter's first pregnancy, casting himself as her responsible benefactor who arranged "towels, disinfectants and nappies."

New York physician Dr. Laszlo Retsagi, M.D., who specializes in internal medicine, said that although historically babies have been delivered at home, there was always a chance of infection.

"Obviously there was a higher mortality rate during delivery," said Dr. Retsagi. "Those who are the fittest survived. There is extra pain during the delivery, creating an uncomfortable sensation and some chances for infection or other things without antibiotics."

Somehow, Elisabeth managed to successfully deliver a baby girl, cutting the umbilical cord herself. She named the baby Kerstin, and from that point, assumed the role of devoted mother, having a new, even stronger reason to survive.

And although Kerstin did not officially exist, her mother secretly recorded her date of birth on a scrap of paper and hid it away.

Ten days after the birth, Josef Fritzl returned to the cellar to see his new daughter/granddaughter. He told Elisabeth it was the beginning of their new family, and that as his new wife, he was expecting more children from her.

Later he would speak of his pride in being a father again, describing his joy at starting a "second proper family."

For he reigned over his subterranean kingdom like a god—and like the ancient Greek deities, he felt it was perfectly permissible to sire children with his daughter.

Kerstin was a sickly baby, suffering cramps and later epilepsy and screaming fits. She would grow up in the claustrophobic, dimly lit one-room dungeon nursed by her mother.

Soon after she was born, Josef Fritzl resumed sexual relations with Elisabeth, in front of their new baby. Growing up, she became used to seeing him in her mother's bed.

"All he cared about was satisfying his lust," a police investigator would later relate, "and keeping the terrible secret of his hidden family."

After Kerstin's birth, Fritzl allowed Elisabeth slightly more freedom within the confines of the dungeon. But he repeatedly warned that any attempt to escape with their baby would turn the dungeon into a deadly gas chamber.

Upstairs, life continued as usual with Rosemarie Fritzl having no idea that she was now a grandmother. The extra demands of a young baby meant her husband was now driving long distances to purchase formula and diapers, so as not to arouse any suspicion in Amstetten.

A couple of months after Kerstin's birth, Elisabeth became pregnant again. Once again, her father would not be there for her, letting her go into labor alone. In late 1989, she delivered a baby boy she named Stefan, carefully noting down his birthday on another piece of paper.

As the 1990s dawned, Austria and the rest of the world were changing fast, as Elisabeth and her two babies languished deep underground in the dark, dank, rat-infested cellar. She had no idea about the fall of the Berlin wall in November 1989, and German unification. And she knew nothing of what was happening in the world, except what her father told her.

In the six years since her disappearance, she had almost been forgotten by her friends, who believed her father's story that she had joined some kind of cult. At their regular Amstetten school reunions, old classmates would sadly reminisce about her before moving on to the next subject.

"Everyone used to chat about what might have happened to Elisabeth," said Gabrielle Heiner, whose brother was in her class. "She suddenly vanished, and no one knew where."

Josef Fritzl was very busy, spending more and more time juggling his two families. But he also found time to regularly visit the Villa Ostende brothel in Linz.

He was well-known in Amstetten, and although not belonging to any church or community group, was a paid-up member of the local fishing group.

"There was never a problem with him," recalled fishing club treasurer Reinhard Kern. "Whether he went fishing or not, how am I to know?"

Since the early 1970s, when Fritzl had rented land from Anton Graf for his vacation campground, the two men had become friends. Graf would occasionally socialize with Fritzl both at the lake and in Amstetten.

"At home he was clearly the lord of the manor," said Graf. "Even at his campground, he was very strict, and his rules had to be followed."

And Fritzl would not accept any excuses for his tenants who broke his rules, evicting them onto the street without a second thought.

"He was inflexible and had no sensitivity," said Graf.

"You were sick, something happened, he didn't care . . . there was a rule . . . and that was it."

Fritzl also loved telling dirty jokes over a beer, and was always the first to laugh.

"He told jokes," remembered Graf. "And not always the cleanest. He laughed loud. A real boom."

Every single part of Josef Fritzl's life was strictly regulated by his obsessive need to be in control. And one by one, as soon as they were old enough, his grown-up children left home to get away from him. Eventually the only one left was his youngest son Josef Jr., who had learning difficulties.

Fritzl put him to work as a houseboy and personal servant, only allowing him to leave the house once a week.

"He had to wait on his father hand and foot," said Chief Inspector Franz Polzer, "and serve him."

In late 1991, Elisabeth became pregnant for the fourth time, the following August giving birth to her second daughter Lisa. With his growing underground family, it was becoming increasingly cramped in the small dungeon, and Josef Fritzl was finding it harder and harder to move around.

Now Elisabeth begged her father for more room for her two toddlers and new baby, so they would not have to witness her being continually raped.

So in 1993, he embarked on an ambitious program to dig a new passageway, connecting the dungeon with the long-forgotten original basement, providing far more space for his subterranean family. He would ultimately create what police would later call a "sophisticated" warren of chambers for sleeping, cooking and washing, and even a rubber-padded cell to rape his daughter in.

But he had no intention of doing the hard work himself, ordering Elisabeth, and later the children when they were old enough, to dig it out with their bare hands. It would take them almost ten years to complete.

From then on, Elisabeth passed much of her time, scooping out the passageway with her hands. Every few nights her father would come and remove the soil, disposing of it in the garden. It was backbreaking work, as there was little air in the dungeon, and it was often unbearably hot in the summer. But somehow Elisabeth carried on for the sake of her children.

A few months after Lisa's birth, Josef Fritzl decided to bring her upstairs to live with the rest of the family. It was becoming more and more expensive to support his two families, and he had discovered that under Austrian law, he would be eligible for a generous state grant if he were to adopt her.

But his dilemma was how to account for the baby's sudden appearance in the outside world. Once again, in his cold and calculating way, he conceived of a monstrous plan to fool everyone.

CHAPTER 11

The Foundlings

On May 19, 1993, Josef Fritzl came down into the cellar, announcing that he was taking Lisa upstairs, so he and Rosemarie could bring her up. Then he gave Elisabeth a pen and paper, and began dictating a new note.

Elisabeth was heartbroken at the prospect of losing her new baby daughter, who weighed just 12 pounds. She had breast-fed her and formed a close bond, as she had with her other two children. But her father was adamant, giving her no choice.

"Dear parents," he made her write, in her soft, flowing handwriting.

> *I hope that you are all healthy. You will probably be shocked to hear from me after all these years, and with a real live surprise, no less. I am leaving you my little daughter Lisa. Take good care of my little girl.*

She wrote that she was still living in the cult with a daughter, Kerstin, and a son, Stefan. But unfortunately they did not approve of her having any more children.

"I breast-fed her for about six-and-a-half-months," her father dictated.

> *And she now drinks her milk from the bottle. She is a good girl, and she eats everything else from the spoon.*
>
> *I will contact you again later, and I beg you not to look for me, because I am doing well. It would be useless, and would only increase my suffering and that of my children. Neither are too many children or education desired there.*
>
> *Elisabeth*

Then, after allowing Elisabeth, Kerstin and Stefan to kiss Lisa good-bye, Josef Fritzl packed the baby in a small cardboard box, bringing her out of the cellar and into the daylight for the first time.

It was the luckiest day of Lisa Fritzl's life.

Later that morning Josef Fritzl brought the cardboard box containing Lisa into the house. He carried it into the living room to show Rosemarie, saying he had just discovered it on the doorstep. Then he read the letter to her, saying that Elisabeth must have abandoned the baby during the night before driving off.

Fritzl then took the letter to Amstetten police headquarters, along with a couple of Elisabeth's old school exercise books, suggesting they be compared by a handwriting expert. He requested a DNA test, explaining that as the baby's grandparents, he and Rosemarie intended to adopt her, but first needed to be certain the baby really was Elisabeth's.

On May 24, five days after Josef Fritzl had brought Lisa up from the cellar, the Amstetten youth welfare office granted him and Rosemarie temporary custody of her during the lengthy adoption process.

Wrote a welfare officer in a report: *Mr. and Mrs. Fritzl have recovered from the initial shock. The Fritzl family is taking loving care of Lisa and wishes to continue caring for her.*

Over the next few years, Amstetten social workers would visit the Fritzl home more than twenty times, reporting "nothing suspicious" about the family, although it was noted that Josef Fritzl was rarely there for the inspections.

On May 20, 1994, a year and a day after bringing Lisa upstairs, the middle-aged couple officially adopted her.

Amstetten welfare officers were so impressed with the caring grandfather that they never bothered with a background check to see if he had a criminal record. Even if they had, it would not have mattered, as all records of his 18-month rape sentence had been officially erased from the records, to protect his privacy.

Now Josef Fritzl began collecting $23 a day in child-care benefits, as well as $230 a month in family benefits. But he would soon learn that it was far more lucrative to foster children than to adopt them, and if he had only fostered Lisa, he would have been entitled to $1,500 a month.

The always-savvy businessman would not make the same mistake again.

Rosemarie Fritzl was delighted to have a new grand daughter to look after, lavishing love on the pale, undernourished baby, who soon put on weight and got stronger. She began taking the little girl out in a stroller around Amstetten, proudly announcing how she and Josef were now bringing up their granddaughter, after Elisabeth had abandoned her.

"Rosemarie told me all about her daughter going off to join the cult," recalled her friend Roswita Zmug. "It seemed incredible to me, but not to her."

The Fritzls' old friend Paul Hoerer says that whenever he visited, Rosemarie seemed "quiet and withdrawn," if her husband was in the same room.

"She didn't tend to say what she was thinking," he remembered. "But whenever Elisabeth was mentioned, she would get up and leave the table."

Elisabeth had been in the damp, dimly lit basement for ten years, and was suffering from a serious anemia and vitamin deficiency herself, and her teeth were starting to rot. She was highly concerned about the effects being locked up was having on 6-year-old Kerstin and 5-- year-old Stefan, who had never seen the sun. She asked her father for vitamin D supplement tablets and an ultraviolet lamp, to stop them from contracting rickets through sunlight deprivation.

After hearing her arguments, Fritzl agreed to bring in the lamp and the vitamins.

"Primarily, [sensory deprivation] acts on the central nervous system," explained Dr. Laszlo Retsagi. "The lack of daylight causes loss of sense of time, creating inappropriate sleep patterns. This leads to a lack of proper sleep, fatigue, headaches, tiredness, dizziness and inappropriate coordination."

There was also so little oxygen from the single ventilation shaft that the prisoners spent most of their time lying down or sitting.

"Lack of fresh oxygen creates problems with clear

thinking," explained Dr. Retsagi. "Which in turn creates problems with clear comprehension and obvious emotional problems."

Elisabeth and her children lived on the packaged food Fritzl bought on his weekly shopping expeditions to supermarkets many miles from Amstetten, to avoid suspicion. Then, under the cover of darkness, he would smuggle food, clothes and toiletries into the cellar.

Elisabeth and the children had no fresh fruit or vegetables to eat, existing solely on frozen or canned products.

"Inappropriate nutrition causes anemia," said Dr. Retsagi. "They were not properly given fresh fruit and vegetables, and all the other nutrients and vitamins young children need, growing up. The lack of appropriate blood cells increases the chance of infection. And when coupled with the lack of sunshine, things become even more complicated."

The only medical care Josef Fritzl did provide were bottles of aspirin, which did nothing to fight the increasing infections they were now contracting.

In 1993, Elisabeth and the children completed the narrow passageway connecting the dungeon to two further rooms. Now Fritzl brought a double bed into the cellar to make things more comfortable for him to rape his daughter.

Later he would bring in a television, so he could then watch soccer games with the children while their mother was preparing a meal. He also built a rubber-padded punishment cell, used for beatings or having sex with Elisabeth.

As soon as her children were old enough, Elisabeth taught them to walk and talk, and later reading and writing. Although she had left school at the first opportunity and was never a great scholar, Elisabeth was determined to give her children the best education possible under the horrific circumstances.

To try to relieve the cellar's interminable boredom, Elisabeth entertained them by making models from cardboard and glue. She also read them fairy stories about princesses and pirates, singing them gentle lullabies to help put them to sleep.

For her children's survival, she carefully maintained the illusion that their life in the cellar was totally normal. She never told them they were prisoners, although she would talk about the world upstairs.

She would explain the difference between day and night, describing the sun, moon and nature. She would try to describe the sound of rain striking the ground during a storm, and the wondrous smell of a green meadow on a summer day.

To little Kerstin and Stefan, the world upstairs seemed like a wondrous fairy-tale heaven compared to the dark lifeless subterranean prison they languished in.

That June, after Elisabeth became pregnant for the fifth time, her father left for another three-week Pattaya pleasure trip. In preparation he had spent weeks stocking the refrigerator with frozen food, and carefully planning every detail of what they would need while he was enjoying himself, thousands of miles away.

But while Josef Fritzl was soaking up the sun on the beach, and indulging himself in prostitutes of both sexes, his pregnant daughter was terrified that if something happened to him, she and the children would be trapped forever.

When he finally returned from Thailand, looking rested and sunburned, he brought gifts for Elisabeth and the children, showing them his vacation photographs.

In early March 1994, Elisabeth delivered a little girl, aided by Kerstin and Stefan. It was a painful birth with only aspirin for medication. And once again she had to cut the umbilical cord herself.

She named the beautiful baby Monika, and Kerstin and Stefan were delighted to have a new baby sister, during the brief time she remained with them.

As landlord, Josef Fritzl had a master key to all the rented apartments. On the days he was unable to go out shopping for his secret family, he let himself into his tenants' apartments and stole food.

Tenant Josef Leitner, who worked construction, said he first noticed how fresh milk, bread, sausages and pasta had gone missing from his fridge while he was out at work. When he mentioned it to the other tenants, they too had similar stories.

Another mystery was their enormous electricity bills, which no one could account for. To save money, their frugal landlord was now diverting their electricity into the cellar.

After receiving one huge quarterly electricity bill, Leitner asked an electrician friend of his for help. But even after all the electrical appliances in his apartment were turned off, his electricity meter continued running.

Although Josef Fritzl banned dogs from the house, Leitner smuggled in an 18-month-old Labrador/husky called Sam. He soon noticed Sam's strange behavior whenever he was near the cellar, as if he sensed something fearful.

"Every time I went on the stairs, the dog tried to run to the cellar and barked," said Leitner. "I was surprised about that, but thought he was just excited about going outside."

Eventually, Fritzl discovered the dog and evicted Leitner.

"He was furious," remembered Leitner. "I came home from work and I couldn't enter my flat. Fritzl had the lock changed. That was enough for me. I called the police."

Leitner finally managed to get his possessions and left forever, but he would never forget Sam's angry reaction to Fritzl, when they came face to face.

"Sam growled at him," he said. "Sam never growled at anybody else."

Just after midnight on Friday, December 16, Josef Fritzl came into the cellar, dictating a third note for Elisabeth to write. This was how she learned for the first time that he was taking Monika upstairs.

I'm really sorry that I had to turn to you again. I hope Lisa is doing well. She must have grown a bit by now. Monika is now nine-and-a-half-months old. She was breast-fed for seven-and-a-half-months. She now eats almost anything but she still likes the bottle best. The hole at the teat has to be a little bigger for her.

He then heartlessly snatched the baby away from her mother, bringing her out of the cellar. Once upstairs, he dropped Monika inside Lisa's stroller at the entranceway to the house.

Then he went outside to a nearby phone box to make a call.

A few minutes later, the phone rang at Ybbsstrasse 40, and Rosemarie answered.

"It's me, don't be angry," whispered Josef Fritzl, disguising his voice into a high whisper, pretending to be Elisabeth. "I just left her at your door. I can't tell you where I'm at."

The call was short and to the point, asking her to take care of the baby, as she could not. Then the line went dead.

Rosemarie was shocked. It was the first contact she had had with her daughter in ten years.

A few hours later, a visibly shaken Rosemarie arrived at Amstetten police headquarters, reporting finding the new baby and Elisabeth's strange phone call. And although she was convinced it had been Elisabeth, she said it was "completely inexplicable" how her daughter could possibly have known their unlisted number, which had been changed since Elisabeth had lived there. An officer duly noted her comments in an official report.

The Amstetten prosecutor's office, the agency responsible for abandoned children, then attempted to find Elisabeth again. But there were no new leads, and unfortunately investigators never bothered to search Josef Fritzl's house, as he was never considered a suspect.

Within weeks, Josef and Rosemarie Fritzl had legally been appointed Monika's foster parents, becoming entitled to a further $1,500 in monthly state benefits.

Just after Christmas, the Austrian media carried the first of many stories about runaway mother Elisabeth Fritzl abandoning her second baby on her parents' doorstep. The baby's grandfather was interviewed by Mark Perry, a reporter for the *Kronen Zeitung* newspaper.

"Our daughter has been [missing] since 1984," Josef Fritzl told him. "And we think she's in the hands of some religious group."

Once again there was great sympathy in Amstetten

for the Fritzls, for selflessly raising their grandchildren, after their irresponsible daughter had run away.

"I thought the grandfather was the perfect head of the family," recalled neighbor Gabrielle Heiner. "Somebody that cared about his children. We used to say how terrible the mother probably was."

Regina Penz, who lived just two houses away, said the abandoned Fritzl babies were the talk of Amstetten.

"Everyone condemned Elisabeth for being an irresponsible bad mother." she said.

CHAPTER 12

Pillar of the Community

In 1995, Josef Fritzl turned 60 years old and was living the good life. He had recently bought a new silver-gray Mercedes-Benz sports car and dressed in expensive tailor-made Italian suits, favoring shiny crocodile shoes.

Most mornings at 5:30 a.m., after spending the night in the dungeon, he would drive through Amstetten to have a close shave and his mustache trimmed at his favorite barber shop in Waidhofner Strasse.

"He was always well-dressed," said a bakery owner in Ybbsstrasse, where Fritzl bought his bread. "When he came into the shop we talked about the news, the weather. He seemed like a normal person."

He was now taking several vacations to Thailand and the Far East each year, as well as spending freely on hookers at his favorite brothels nearer home. But in Amstetten he and his wife were considered well-respected citizens.

He was now assiduously cultivating influential friends in high places, to help oil the wheels of his increasingly ambitious real estate deals. One of them was Leopold Styetz, the vice mayor of Lasberg, a small town near Amstetten, who he occasionally socialized with.

"For me," recalled Styetz, "Sepp seemed an intelligent and successful man."

Apart from the two houses in Amstetten, Fritzl also owned properties in St. Polten and Waidhofen an der Ybbs, which were also rented out to tenants. These provided the cover necessary for his twice-weekly long-distance shopping trips, buying food, diapers and furniture for his dungeon family.

Although he appeared to be a successful property entrepreneur, investigators would later discover he had fraudulently re-mortgaged his five rental properties several times over. For a time, he would keep one step ahead of the banks, but eventually they would catch up with him.

That year Alfred Dubanovsky, who had been in Elisabeth Fritzl's class at school, moved into Ybbsstrasse 40. For the next twelve years he rented a small room just a few feet above the dungeon.

Before he was allowed to move in, his new landlord read him a strict set of house rules that had to be observed.

"Such a strange guy," recalled Dubanovsky, who worked at a local gas station. "Only he alone was allowed to go into the cellar. He told us that the cellar was protected with a sophisticated alarm system, and that whoever went there would have their contract cancelled without notice. He was very strict about that."

Josef Fritzl had divided the first floor of the large house into eight apartments, which he rented out. He and his family occupied the top two storys.

Over the years he lived there, Dubanovsky tried to avoid his landlord whenever possible, but noticed his frequent visits to the cellar.

"He went there almost every day," he said. "I thought it was a bit strange, but I didn't find it suspicious."

Dubanovsky's bedroom window looked out onto the back garden, and some nights he watched Fritzl ferrying food and other supplies from his car into the cellar with a wheelbarrow.

"But I never saw him bring any out," he said. "And it was always at night."

Another tenant, who moved into the house several years later, told *Der Spiegel* magazine that Fritzl's youngest son Josef Jr. also had a key to the cellar.

"He acted as though he was the building's superintendent," said the tenant, only identified as Christian B, "but he never did very much. He had a key to the cellar."

Sabine Kirschbichler, 25, who lived on the second floor with her brother Thomas in a $675-a-month apartment from 2001 to 2003, confirmed that Josef Jr. had a key, and frequently went down to the cellar.

"He was the caretaker," she said. "If anything was broken, he would go straight to the cellar to fetch a replacement."

According to Sabine, Fritzl's portly son, then in his mid-thirties, was usually drunk.

"He always had a bottle in his hand," said Sabine, "beer or wine."

Alfred Dubanovsky had always been surprised that Fritzl's son still lived at home, and was only allowed out of the house once a week.

"I certainly found that very strange," he said.

Some nights, Dubanovsky would hear mysterious "knocking and banging" noises coming from the cellar, as well as objects being dropped. But when he asked what they were, Fritzl said it was the heating system, offering to move him to a larger apartment upstairs, but Dubanovsky declined.

Other than relatives and a few close friends, the Fritzls

had few visitors. But on one occasion Fritzl introduced Dubanovsky to a plumber, who had been allowed into the cellar to help install a heavy toilet system.

Lina Angermeier, who rented a small apartment on the first floor, said everyone knew about Elisabeth Fritzl running away and abandoning her babies.

"That was no secret," she told *Spiegel*. "We thought she was a bad mother who shirked her maternal responsibilities. You felt sorry for the Fritzl family, because of their bad fortune."

When Angermeier moved into her apartment, which overlooked the inner courtyard, Rosemarie Fritzl told her there was no tenant storage space in the cellar, and that her husband never allowed tenants to go anywhere near it.

During the time she lived there, Angermeier always thought the Fritzls a happy family.

"They all seemed to get along well," she recalled. "The other kids came to visit a lot. Josef and Rosemarie Fritzl were very loving, and doted over their grandchildren. Elisabeth was always portrayed as the black sheep of the family."

That summer, Elisabeth Fritzl became pregnant for the fifth time. And on April 29, 1996, she delivered a set of male twins—Alex and Michael. Once again, their father was absent, apparently finding the idea of childbirth distasteful.

Soon after birth, Michael developed severe respiratory problems, and Elisabeth desperately battled to save his life, without any medical supplies. She pleaded with her father to take the baby to the hospital, but he refused, saying, "What will be, will be." Then after three long days, he died in his mother's arms, as Kerstin and Stefan looked on helplessly.

Josef Fritzl was furious. He picked up his dead son's body and stormed over to the incinerator, used to dispose of the cellar garbage, and threw it in.

Twelve years later, he would admit burning baby Michael's body, explaining that he had wanted to "get rid of it."

Although the terrible toll on Kerstin and Stefan of witnessing their baby brother's death may never be known, somehow their mother rose above it to survive. After Michael's death, Josef Fritzl relaxed his regime even further. Each new baby had increased his control over Elisabeth, who now obeyed his every command for the sake of her children. He cunningly exploited this, bringing in a radio, television and a VCR. To brighten up the dingy cellar, he smuggled in old carpets, chairs, tables and second-hand kitchen utensils. He even acquired an aquarium for 7-year-old Stefan, who would spend hours just staring at the fish swimming around in it.

Over the next several years, Josef Fritzl completed several more rooms, providing a kitchen, a small lavatory with sink and makeshift shower, and two bedrooms for Elisabeth and her children to sleep in.

Elisabeth was now spending three hours a day educating her children. Although she had left school at 15, she was teaching Kerstin and Stefan basic math, history and geography, using textbooks her father bought.

And late at night, after their jailer had satisfied himself and finally left, Elisabeth would tell Kerstin and Stefan about the outside world, describing her own childhood before she had been brought down into the cellar, always careful never to let them know they were prisoners.

Their new television, which was now on day and night, had suddenly opened up the children's narrow world. But they had no grasp of reality outside the cellar, so it was as if the television pictures they saw came from another planet. There was absolutely nothing for them to distinguish news programs from Hollywood fantasy movies.

Their father now began turning his cellar visits into grotesquely distorted family occasions. He'd arrive bearing small presents for the children, as well as the sexy silk lingerie for their mother that so pleased him. He would buy Elisabeth's underwear and evening gowns mail order, using a credit card he'd registered in her name. And over the years, dozens of parcels would arrive at Ybbsstrasse 40, addressed to Elisabeth Fritzl, somehow never attracting any attention.

After Elisabeth had dressed up for him, her children would retreat into their bedroom while he forced her to view hardcore pornographic tapes on the VCR. He would then force her to reenact his favorite perverted scenes in a special rubber-padded room.

Afterwards, Elisabeth would go into the kitchen to cook dinner on the ancient oven he'd installed, as they discussed Kerstin and Stefan's upbringing. Then after dinner, while Elisabeth cleaned up, he would settle down in front of the television with his children, watching soccer matches, martial arts movies or Formula 1 racing.

On special occasions, he would show them photographs of their siblings upstairs, proudly recounting how well they were doing at school, and the various exciting trips they had been taking.

Then early the next morning he'd leave, going upstairs to resume his other life with his other family.

* * *

Living their lives in artificial light in such a confined space affected the children's balance and coordination. Stefan, who grew to be 5 feet, 9 inches, would be permanently crippled after years of never being able to stand up straight because of the low ceilings.

They all suffered unimaginable sensory deprivation, as well as vitamin deficiencies and problems with their immune systems.

The four rooms they eventually occupied were connected by long narrow passageways, just two feet wide. There was little oxygen and the damp cellar walls were covered in mildew, causing continuing fungal infections.

It was a miserable existence, but despite the overwhelming odds, Elisabeth always tried to make life exciting for her children. To relieve the boredom, she taught them games, encouraging them to decorate the gloomy rooms to make them more livable. Together they painted a yellow snail with a green shell, purple octopuses, flowers and fish on the dirty white bathroom tiles. And they covered the damp ceilings with colorful decals of the sun and stars in the heavens.

But the children had never seen anything outside the cellar with their own eyes, having to rely on book illustrations or digital television images.

On August 3, 1997, after forcing Elisabeth to write yet another note, Josef Fritzl brought Michael's 15-month-old twin brother Alexander upstairs, depositing him on the doorstep. Once again he went through the charade of his daughter thoughtlessly abandoning yet another baby for him and his wife to raise.

"When Elisabeth's third child was laid at the door, we asked Sepp if maybe he shouldn't try to find out about this sect," recalled his sister-in-law Christine. "His answer was, 'No point.'"

Horst Herlbauer, who is married to Fritzl's second-oldest daughter Rosemarie, said the family always believed Elisabeth had run away.

"That was the truth to us," he explained, "and we didn't question it, even when some of her children appeared and were adopted into the family."

Once again the story was reported in the *Kronen Zeitung* newspaper, and Elisabeth's irresponsible behavior was the subject of much discussion in Amstetten.

The authorities also did little to try to find Elisabeth. And after another routine inspection of Ybbsstrasse 40 by Amstetten social workers, Josef Fritzl was soon receiving another $1,500-a-month government check for his new foster son.

By all accounts, life for the three children lucky enough to have escaped the cellar was good. Their doting grandmother Rosemarie took good care of them, and their grandfather always insisted they call them "Mama" and "Papa."

Lisa and Monika went to the local school in Amstetten, where they were reportedly excellent students. Monika had suffered from a congenital heart condition which had required surgery, but was now fully recovered.

Upstairs, they lived a mirror life of their unfortunate brother and sister two floors below, having no idea that Kerstin and Stefan even existed. They dressed well and were allowed to have friends over to the house to use the new swimming pool that their grandfather had recently built on the roof.

They studied different musical instruments, played ice hockey and other sports, took summer vacations to Italy and Greece with Rosemarie.

"She made a lot of sacrifices," said Lina Anger-meier, "for the sake of her grandchildren."

Neighbor Regina Penz was always impressed by how well Rosemarie Fritzl was raising her new set of children, though she pitied her for the strain it must have caused.

"Frau Fritzl already had seven children," she said. "And now she had to bring up grandchildren as well. Terrible."

In summer 1996, Josef Fritzl sold his boarding house at Lake Mondsee, giving up the campsite after almost twenty-five years. To celebrate, he went to the Munich Oktoberfest with his old friend Paul Hoerer, who later stayed a couple of days at the Fritzl house with his girl-friend Andrea Schmitt.

Hoerer remembers his friend being the perfect host, entertaining them by his roof garden pool, immaculately set with white marble tiles.

"We got on really well," he remembered. "He was great company and seemed to be the picture-book head of the family. Looking back, I suppose it was a bit strange that the only garden we were ever allowed to use was the one on the roof."

Hoerer said he was aware the cellar was "totally out of bounds," but had no reason to go there.

"We never went down to the garden," he said. "But sat on the terrace garden, looking down. I always thought it was a wonderful family. The children were well-mannered and so well-behaved."

After dinner, the two friends adjourned to Fritzl's

media room, watching his favorite Bugs Bunny and Tom and Jerry television cartoons, which made him laugh hysterically.

Fritzl's grown-up daughter Gabrielle spent three years living at Ybbsstrasse 40 with her husband Jergen Helm. During that time, Helm got close to his father-in-law, often sharing an evening drink and a chat on the roof terrace by the pool.

"There was always a relaxed atmosphere," he told the German newspaper *Heute*. "There was never any indication of anything wrong."

He said he had been in the cellar on at least one occasion, never noticing anything untoward.

"It was scattered with junk," he recalled. "And I had no idea that a few meters away this family were living."

CHAPTER 13

A Double Life

Even though he kept his daughter Elisabeth as his personal sex slave, Josef Fritzl's libido was insatiable. He had discovered Viagra and other similar prescription drugs, and his esoteric tastes in deviant sex were becoming stranger and stranger. Villa Ostende owner Peter Stolz was becoming increasingly concerned about his long-time customer's demands.

"He was a strange, stingy character," remembered Stolz. "He liked trips to the dungeon"—the brothel's underground lair—"with young girls he had selected personally."

One of the few Villa Ostende girls still willing to accept him as a client told London's *Sun* newspaper how he liked to tie her to a cross with manacles in the dungeon. The 36-year-old blonde prostitute, who charged Fritzl $220 an hour, said he was often violent and bad-tempered, punching her during sex.

"I was hired by him many times," she told a reporter, refusing to give her name. "And he was sick beyond imagination."

She said he especially liked her because she was young, plump and submissive.

"I had to call him 'teacher,'" she remembered, "and was not allowed to engage in conversation with him.

He would pay to have sex inside the brothel dungeon, which I hated. It was dark and sinister, but his favorite place.

"Once I asked him about his family and he told me, 'I have none.' I thought he was a lonely man."

By Christmas 1998, Josef Fritzl seemed to have everything under control. He now lived his complicated double life with military precision, getting an extra thrill out of beating the system for thousands of dollars every month in government benefits.

He felt so secure, he was now planning another month-long "boys' trip" to Thailand, to be immediately followed by a two-week Italian vacation. In anticipation of being away so long, once again he began stockpiling large amounts of food in a spare room in the cellar.

In the weeks up to Christmas, he had driven to various supermarkets around a fifty-mile radius of Amstetten. He often shopped at the Metro superstore in Linz, near the Villa Ostende, refueling afterwards at the gas station next door.

"He went shopping almost every week," recalled a gas pump attendant, who served him regularly over a fifteen-year period. "Sometimes his wife was with him."

The attendant, who wished to remain anonymous, said Fritzl was stingy, and never left a tip.

After his shopping expeditions, he would arrive home between 10 and 11 at night, using his wheelbarrow to transfer the large plastic bags full of groceries across the garden and into the cellar.

Alfred Dubanovsky would later claim to have seen Rosemarie Fritzl assist him on several occasions.

"The amount was far too much for Josef, his wife

and the three kids still at home," said Dubanovsky. "Rosemarie must have noticed. In fact, she often helped him unload things."

Dubanovsky said another tenant also once expressed surprise about the enormous amounts of food regularly being taken into the cellar.

"Looking back," he said, "I suppose this must have been shortly before he went on holiday."

Walter Werner, who lived near the Fritzls for eleven years, also observed the mysterious food runs into the cellar, but never said anything.

"In retrospect," he would later say, "I have to say I found it strange that they used to carry so many groceries into the house, they needed a wheelbarrow to transport them."

Over the Christmas holidays, Josef Fritzl held his annual family reunion at Ybbsstrasse 40. Ironically, he had a sentimental streak, delighting in celebrating birthdays and holidays separately with both his upstairs and downstairs families, although they might have been on different planets.

Over the holiday period, all the grown-up Fritzl children returned with their spouses for a lavish festive meal. As usual, the family patriarch sat at the head of the table, presiding over everything. Sometimes the conversation turned to Elisabeth and where she could possibly be.

"We went back for family occasions," said Fritzl's son-in-law Horst Herlbauer. "Josef seemed to be a normal dad and family man. He was always working hard [at] his job or on the house. There never appeared to be any problems at home."

But although Herlbauer found his father-in-law "outgoing" and "friendly," other members of the family did not. Rosemarie Fritzl's younger sister Christine had detested her brother-in-law ever since his 1967 rape imprisonment, and she made no secret of it when they met at family reunions.

When Fritzl would mock his wife at the dinner table, saying, "Chubby women are below my standard," Christine would gamely reply, "Better to be chubby than bald."

It had been after one of these exchanges that he had secretly gone to Vienna for an expensive hair transplant.

Throughout family meals, he would crack off-color jokes in front of the children, embarrassing everyone as he laughed heartily. Rosemarie was often the butt of his savage humor, and he appeared to take pleasure in publicly humiliating her.

"He was relaxed and sociable with everyone in the family apart from Rosi," said Christine. "He used to tell her off in front of the others. The worst things were his crude, dirty jokes, which he used to laugh loudly about. This was embarrassing for everyone, because we all knew that the two of them hadn't had sex for twenty years. He would always say, 'My wife is much too chubby for me.'"

Then later, after his family had left, he'd sneak down into the cellar to celebrate Christmas with Elisabeth and his secret family, bearing cakes and little presents. One year he even arrived with a small Christmas tree, which Kerstin and Stefan decorated.

On Tuesday, January 6, 1998, Josef Fritzl flew to Pattaya, Thailand, for a month-long beach vacation. Before leaving, he had told Elisabeth he would be back on February 3, leaving enough food for her and the children. As he'd left, he'd repeated his warning that any attempt to escape would release deadly gas into the cellar.

Paul Hoerer, his girlfriend Andrea Schmitt and stepfather Rainer Wieczorak accompanied him. Over the next four weeks, while Elisabeth and the children languished underground, Fritzl sunbathed, swam in the deep blue sea and took boat trips to the nearby island Ko Lan. Then at night he went off by himself, indulging in sex with both male and female Thai hookers.

"He traveled alone without his wife. He told me she had to look after the children," said Hoerer.

"The first time he really admitted to me that he was not the perfect family man was in Thailand," Hoerer recalled. "He obviously liked women, and good-looking women at that. But I know his wife was not his type."

Hoerer had brought along a camcorder, shooting video of Josef Fritzl enjoying himself. The paunchy senior citizen is seen lying on the beach, wearing a skimpy zebra-striped Speedo and receiving a back massage from a young Thai masseur. After the massage, he gets up, walks toward the camera and gives a peace sign with a big smile on his face.

In another shot, he's wearing a smart black-and-white shirt for dinner. He mugs for the camera, as he greedily stuffs a large knuckle of roast ham into his mouth.

"Once we were at a market in Pattaya," said Hoerer, "and he didn't know that I was behind him when he bought an evening dress and underwear for a thin woman. It would not have fit his wife."

When Fritzl turned around and saw Hoerer filming him, he was furious. Later, when he had calmed down, Hoerer asked who the frilly underwear was for.

"He then admitted he had a woman on the side,"

said Hoerer, "and asked me to keep it secret and not to tell his wife."

Hoerer's girlfriend Andrea remembers Fritzl spending much time on the trip buying children's presents.

"He had several carrier bags filled with things," she said. "And I remember thinking, 'What a lot of presents for just three children.'"

Rainer Wieczorak, who was also on the trip, rarely saw Fritzl during the entire vacation.

"I need to go there because the warm climate is much better for my health," he said. "But Josef had other interests. While we would all sit around the hotel bar enjoying a few quiet drinks, he was off on his own."

Hoerer said his friend was very secretive about his nights in Pattaya, and whenever street girls approached Fritzl to offer sex, he "blocked" them, saying he was not interested.

But his friends all knew he trawled the sex bars every night, though they never mentioned it for fear of making him angry.

"He always went off on his own at night," said Andrea. "I believe he went to some of the clubs."

And when he finally reappeared the next morning, he looked exhausted, spending the day recovering.

"He was usually sleeping things off during the day," said Wieczorak, "having a massage on the beach and a late breakfast."

Josef Fritzl also bought himself expensive gifts in Pattaya, including several pairs of flashy crocodile shoes and some handmade shirts.

During the flight back, Fritzl told his friends it had been one of the greatest vacations of his life.

"He enjoyed it so much," said Schmitt, "that he said when he got back he was going to go on holiday again to Italy. That meant he would have been on holiday about six weeks in total."

On March 2, 1998—almost fourteen years after Josef Fritzl had first lured Elisabeth into the cellar—a 10-year-old girl named Natascha Kampusch disappeared on the way to her school. The troubled young girl from a broken home, who was the same age as Kerstin, was seen being dragged into a white minibus near her home in Vienna.

After Natascha's disappearance, a massive police hunt was launched to try to find her. Among the many hundreds of minivan owners questioned was a 35-year-old communications technician named Wolfgang Priklopil, who told police he'd been using his van to transport rubbish the morning of the kidnapping and was allowed to go.

In fact, Priklopil had become obsessed with Natascha, fantasizing about kidnapping her and turning her into his sex slave. Just like Josef Fritzl, in the months leading up to the abduction, he had constructed an elaborate dungeon in the cellar of his family house in Strasshof an der Nordbahn in Lower Austria.

The house had been built by his grandfather Oskar Priklopil, who had later converted the cellar into a nuclear bomb shelter during the Cold War. When Oskar died in 1984, his grandson Wolfgang inherited the house.

Then, in the mid-1990s, Wolfgang, who lived with his mother, began constructing an underground "bunker" for his victim, as yet unselected.

Like Josef Fritzl, Priklopil was a highly organized and meticulous man. The parallels between the two, who were living within a hundred miles of each other, were astonishing. As Fritzl had done years earlier, Priklopil spent years constructing a series of concrete-lined narrow tunnels and passageways. He installed a bathroom with a tiny sink and toilet, connecting the plumbing to the main house, as the electricity also was. He soundproofed his dungeon, which was only ventilated by an air system that he controlled from above.

This tiny dungeon, measuring just 54 square feet, would be Natascha Kampusch's world for more than eight years. It contained a bed, a ladder and little else. For the first six months of her captivity, the little girl was never allowed to leave, being told by her kidnapper that the door and windows were booby-trapped with high explosives, set to go off if she tried to escape.

That March, Natascha Kampusch's abduction was big news in Austria. And the chances are that Elisabeth and the children saw news reports on the television, flickering day and night in their prison, just 100 miles due west of hers.

CHAPTER 14

His Underground Kingdom

In late 1999, two Amstetten fire inspectors arrived at Ybbsstrasse 40 for a routine fire inspection. An unfazed Josef Fritzl led them downstairs into the cellar heating room, only yards away from the secret dungeon entrance. The officials carefully inspected the boiler furnace, where, three years earlier, he had tossed baby Michael's body. The inspectors found that it met official requirements, failing to notice the well-hidden cellar entrance behind some shelving.

Fritzl must have breathed a sigh of relief as he led them back upstairs, knowing that his secret was safe for the time being.

Though approaching 65, Josef Fritzl showed no signs of slowing down. He was now consumed with an ambitious plan to build a three-story apartment housing project, with offices and an underground garage in the Amstetten town center. He had already raised $1.5 million in loans, using his five rental properties as collateral.

But he ran into problems, after listing Elisabeth on all the deeds as a tax dodge. His Austrian bankers now refused to re-mortgage the properties, as his missing daughter was technically a sitting tenant, making it impossible to sell if he defaulted on the loan.

To get around this, he pretended to need the money

for a new ladies' underwear business, to be run from his home on the Internet. But, although he eventually got the loans, the project never materialized, after angry residents took legal action to prevent it, saying it would ruin the neighborhood.

Most afternoons, Josef Fritzl visited the James Dean Club, which catered to an older clientele. Located at Waidhofner Strasse 56, just a short walk from his home, he would stroll into the club with a big grin, always greeting the pretty Slavic hostesses by their first names.

"What's new?" he'd ask, as he stood at the bar, ordering coffee with two milks. And for the next several hours he would hold court, chatting with old school friends and flirting with the waitresses. He also used the club for business meetings, never dancing with the miniskirted hostesses or drinking alcohol.

But there were other types of clubs around Amstetten that he also patronized.

Local builder Paul Stocker first met Fritzl in 1997, when he came to view a house Stocker was selling. Although the deal never materialized, the two men, both in their sixties, became friends. They occasionally met for a "boys' night out" at the Caribik swingers' club, a few miles outside Amstetten.

The club's website boasts of its "small dungeon and guestrooms for overnight stays." The entrance fee is $115 for couples and $15 for women.

"Fritzl told me someone of our age can have a lot of fun with sex," recalled Stocker. "He said you needed to take three tablets—Viagra, Levitra and Cialis. The pills kick in one after the other and you can go for it like a bull."

A week later, Stocker was at the club when he claims Josef Fritzl walked in with his wife Rosemarie.

"They looked just like an old pair that you might see sitting on a bench feeding pigeons," he said. "I was speechless when I realized who it was."

According to Stocker, Fritzl sent Rosemarie to stand in a corner, before hooking up with a young woman. Then they had sex by the tree-lined pool, as his wife looked on.

"He treated [Rosemarie] like a dog," said Stocker. "She had to sit in a corner and watch, as he did stuff with a young woman. I think it's fair to say he made a good job of it. Then he left with his totally humiliated and degraded wife and went home."

In 2000, the Fritzls celebrated their 44th wedding anniversary with a small family party. After so many years in such a turbulent marriage, Rosemarie still kept up the pretense of living an idyllic family life. She played the part of happy wife and mother to perfection, becoming her husband's unwitting accomplice.

She devoted herself to bringing up Lisa, now 8, Monika, 6, and Alexander, 4. Amstetten social workers, who regularly interviewed the children, were most impressed with their excellent upbringing.

One report noted how the grandparents went to great pains "to encourage the children in many ways." It lauded the Fritzls for providing the children with "books and cassettes from the city library," as well as facilitating their "children's gymnastics."

"[The Fritzls] are very loving with their children," the report concluded.

"To the outside world they seemed like a great family," said neighbor Anita Lachinger. "She cooked and cleaned for them . . . she loved them."

Most days Rosemarie Fritzl, now in her mid-sixties, drove the children to their ice hockey league games or classical music lessons. Lisa played flute in the school orchestra, while Monika and Alexander studied trumpet. Rosemarie would also take various classes, including one on the art of napkin folding, at a nearby crafts shop.

Rosemarie brought the three children up to believe that their mother Elisabeth had abandoned them, after running away to join a religious sect. Little Alexander became so terrified that his mother would come and kidnap him from his bed, he almost stopped talking.

"Rosemarie was desperate to give the children a normal start in life, with a proper mom and dad," said a family friend. "She was deeply hurt and embarrassed about Elisabeth supposedly running off."

One of the children's music teachers was "amazed" at her strength, only once seeing her break down and cry, when she told him how her daughter had run away and joined a cult.

When Lisa started school, her teachers were so alarmed when she referred to the elderly Fritzls as "Mama and Papa," that the couple was summoned to school.

"The teachers told Rosemarie she had to come clean," said the friend, "or the children would be totally messed up when they discovered the truth later."

So in summer 2000, Rosemarie hired a child psychologist to counsel the children.

"Then she threw a party to make them feel positive about the new family setup," said the friend. "From then on she and [Josef] were 'Omi and Opi'" (Grandma and Grandpa).

Rosemarie also determined that the children should have a religious upbringing, organizing their first communions.

But behind closed doors, Josef Fritzl was the same bullying dictator he had always been. Once Rosemarie confided to her friend that Josef was so domineering that he terrified Lisa and Alexander, making their lives miserable.

At the age of 11, Lisa, who bore an uncanny resemblance to her mother Elisabeth, persuaded Fritzl to send her to the prestigious Kloster's private girls' school, run by Catholic nuns.

The two younger children went to local schools, where they became well-behaved model students, always getting good grades. Their proud grandmother became an active member of the parent–teacher association.

Soon after starting Kloster's, just outside Amstetten, Lisa told her new classmates how her mother had left her on her grandparents' doorstep when she was a baby.

"We know Lisa and Monika were foundling children," a former classmate told the London *Mirror* newspaper, "and had both been abandoned at the front door of the Fritzl home when they were born, almost like a Bible story. Lisa told us her story at the start of school, but we never mentioned it again out of respect and politeness."

But several years later, when Alexander started high school, he told his classmates a different story.

"He always told us his mother was dead," remembered classmate Verena Huber.

That summer, Josef Fritzl hosted twenty-five members of his family at his favorite Linz restaurant, Bratwurstglockerl. After enjoying a hearty meal of traditional Austrian cuisine, Fritzl, who was in an unusually good mood that day, took an official family photograph outside the restaurant.

In the photograph Rosemarie is all smiles, sitting next to her grandson Alexander. Lisa and Monika stand to her right, surrounded by the other members of the extended Fritzl family.

* * *

In February 2002, Elisabeth became pregnant for the seventh time. She had been down in the cellar for eighteen years, and was suffering from serious vitamin deficiency, malnourishment and acute emotional stress. Although she was only in her mid-thirties, her teeth were falling out because of gum disease, and her once flame red hair had turned grey.

But for Kerstin and Stefan's sake, she never complained, realizing that she had to be strong for the family to survive. Even her father grudgingly admired his daughter's fortitude in some kind of twisted way. He would later talk of her strength, and how she had caused him "almost no problems" during this time, never complaining even as her teeth fell out one by one.

After she became pregnant for the last time, her father no longer demanded sex, as he was no longer attracted to her. Investigators believe he may have turned his attention to 13-year-old Kerstin, and started grooming the frail, sickly girl to take over her mother's duties.

On December 16, 2002, Elisabeth delivered a little boy she named Felix. Soon after his birth, his father came into the dungeon, announcing that this time the baby boy would remain underground, as Rosemarie could not handle another baby.

Then he magnanimously brought a washing machine into the cellar, so Elizabeth would no longer have to wash her and the children's clothes by hand.

A few months later, Josef Fritzl dictated another letter for Elisabeth to write, announcing that she had given birth to a baby boy the previous December. Once again Fritzl mailed the letter from a postbox far away from Amstetten, providing no further clues of his daughter's whereabouts.

CHAPTER 15

Losing Control

In summer 2003, Josef Fritzl's meticulously constructed world began to come apart at the seams. When his much-vaunted Amstetten housing complex fell apart, he was left owing banks more than $1 million. Now facing bankruptcy, he was having difficulty maintaining his extravagant lifestyle and supporting two separate families.

Once again, investigators believe, he resorted to arson, just as he was suspected of having done twenty-one years earlier at Mondsee Lake.

Late at night on August 22, a suspicious fire broke out in one of his first-floor rental apartments. Police and firefighters arrived at the house to discover Fritzl and his son Josef Jr., fighting the fire together. A female tenant, who had been in the apartment when the fire started, was taken to the hospital for smoke inhalation.

A few days later, after Fritzl claimed $15,000 from his insurance company for the damage, two police officers were sent to investigate for suspected arson.

"It was started in two places—a classic sign of arson," a source close to the investigation later said. "But despite that, the officers only carried out a brief investigation."

Once again, Josef Fritzl's secret dungeon went unnoticed.

That Christmas, another mysterious fire broke out at the house—this time in the Fritzl family's third-floor apartment. A television in the children's room burst into flames, Fritzl later informed authorities, before claiming $4,500 from his insurance company.

Several months later, he claimed a further $1,500, reporting that one of his electric meters had caught fire.

Neither of these two fires were investigated, and the insurance company paid him a total of almost $20,000, without any further questions.

On Saturday, April 9, 2005, Josef Fritzl turned 70, and Rosemarie threw a big birthday party on the roof garden in his honor. Several of his friends attended, including Paul Hoerer and Andrea Schmitt. Of his thirteen surviving children, ten came, including all the grown-up ones who had left home, as well as Lisa, Monika and Alexander. But downstairs Elisabeth and his three captive children heard nothing, remaining unaware of the festivities.

"We sat on the terrace," said Paul Hoerer, "and had a really nice evening."

Three weeks later, Sunday, August 28, marked the 21st anniversary of Elisabeth's imprisonment. That day, like so many thousands of others, came and went in the dark, decaying underground bunker.

Elisabeth and her three children's lives had no measurable landmarks. There was no perceivable day and night to mark time, or routines to follow. The only punctuations in their shadow lives were rotten teeth falling out, or their never-ending infections, for which the only medication available was aspirin.

They were getting weaker by the day, having nothing to look forward to. Even a murderer serving a life sentence can mark off the days on a prison wall until parole, but these four captives—who had done nothing except to be sired by Josef Fritzl—did not even have that to anticipate.

Now officially retired and collecting his state pension, Josef Fritzl was showing signs of slowing down. Although Viagra and other drugs still powered his out-of-control libido, he was no longer as menacing to Elisabeth as he had once seemed. And she was slowly beginning to assert herself, constantly pressing him for better conditions for her and the children.

Escape had never been an option. Elisabeth had always believed his threats of booby-trapping the cellar with poisonous gas. And her children never realized they were prisoners, or that their lives were anything but normal.

At 15, Stefan had grown into a handsome young man, but the terrible conditions in the cellar had stunted his normal development. He was too tall to stand erect without scraping his head on the ceiling, often finding it easier to crawl around on his hands and knees.

Elisabeth and her children all had terrible physical posture, and were anemic with severely challenged immune systems. Never seeing sunlight or breathing fresh air was starting to take a terrible toll on them.

There were also many unanswered questions lingering in Elisabeth's mind about the medical repercussions of incest.

As Felix grew into a toddler, he bonded with Stefan, the two inventing their own language, largely composed of animal-like growls and coos.

The little boy would spend hours each day watching

the color television, desperately clutching a stuffed teddy bear his father had given him. Across the room, his brother would stare blankly at his aquarium.

Sickly since birth, Kerstin now possibly faced the unspeakable trauma of succeeding her mother as Josef Fritzl's sex slave.

In 2006, Josef and Rosemarie Fritzl passed another milestone, celebrating their golden wedding anniversary. The town of Amstetten honored its model family with a special party, where the mayor and a succession of town dignitaries paid gushing tributes to the elderly couple.

The 71-year-old retiree beamed with pride as he and his wife were lauded as devoted parents and grandparents, who had selflessly brought up their runaway daughter's abandoned children.

Although considered a successful local property magnate, that was far from the truth. Fritzl was sinking into debt, and even after managing to have Elisabeth's name removed from his property deeds, he owed an estimated $1.5 million to various banks.

But to the arrogant septuagenarian, appearances were everything—an impeccably dressed paragon of virtue, he still proudly drove around Amstetten in his top-of-the-line Mercedes.

He reserved Saturdays for Rosemarie and his three "grandchildren," Lisa, Monika and Alexander. Saturday afternoons he would take Alexander to watch the Amstetten soccer team play, and afterwards they would all enjoy a pizza dinner at the Casa Verona Italian restaurant in Karl-Benz-Strasse, a few blocks away from their home. To the owner, Wael Saham, the Fritzls seemed the perfect family.

The iconic Amstetten Police mugshot of Josef Fritzl, taken the night of his arrest, is the very personification of evil.

AFP/Getty Images

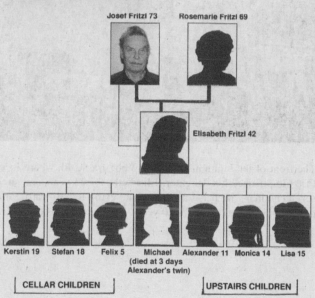

Josef Fritzl 73   Rosemarie Fritzl 69

Elisabeth Fritzl 42

Kerstin 19   Stefan 18   Felix 5   Michael (died at 3 days Alexander's twin)   Alexander 11   Monica 14   Lisa 15

CELLAR CHILDREN   UPSTAIRS CHILDREN

The Fritzl family tree.   *Gail Freund and Will Crompton*

The front of the infamous house at Ybbestrasse 40, where Josef Fritzl imprisoned his daughter, Elisabeth, for 24 years and sired seven children with her. Later he would claim to have earlier imprisoned his mother there for 20 years, before taking his daughter.

Johannes Simon/Getty Images

Elisabeth Fritzl's best friend at school, Christa Woldrich (nee Goetzinger), released a tribute CD to raise money for the Fritzl family, using a teenage photograph of her friend before her kidnapping.

Christa Woldrich

The entrance to the dungeon was so well hidden that Amstetten Police had to bring Josef Fritzl back to the house to open it for them.

SID Lower Austria via Getty Images

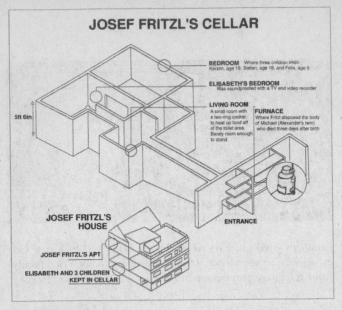

JOSEF FRITZL'S CELLAR

BEDROOM Where three children slept:
Kerstin, age 19, Stefan, age 18, and Felix, age 5

ELISABETH'S BEDROOM
Was soundproofed with a TV and video recorder

LIVING ROOM
A small room with
a two-ring cooker
to heat up food off
of the toilet area.
Barely room enough
to stand.

FURNACE
Where Fritzl disposed the body
of Michael (Alexander's twin)
who died three days after birth

5ft 6in

**JOSEF FRITZL'S
HOUSE**

JOSEF FRITZL'S APT

**ELISABETH AND 3 CHILDREN
KEPT IN CELLAR**

ENTRANCE

A diagram of the cellar.   *Gail Freund and Will Crompton*

A view of the cellar, showing
one of the cramped corridors
where Elisabeth Fritzl and her
children existed in deplorable
conditions.

*SID Lower Austria
via Getty Images*

The dungeon bathroom, which the children decorated with stars and paintings in an effort to make it more homey.

SID Lower Austria via Getty Images

The Fritzl house was in the middle of one of Amstetten's busiest thoroughfares, but it never attracted any suspicions during the quarter century Elisabeth and her children languished there.

John MacDougall/AFP/Getty Images

Lower Austrian Police Chief Franz Polzer holds up a photograph of Josef Fritzl during his first press conference the day after the arrest.

*Markus Leodolter/
AFP/Getty Images*

Dr. Albert Reiter (left) of Amstetten Hospital was immediately suspicious of Josef Fritzl's story about his daughter Elisabeth joining a cult and called in the police. Sitting to his right is Mauer Hospital Chief Berthold Kepplinger and Fritzl family civil attorney, Christoph Herbst.

Dieter Nagl/AFP/Getty Images

Lisa Fritzl, 15, the oldest of the upstairs children, is the image of her mother, Elisabeth, as a teenager.

Dieter Nagl/AFP/Getty Images

The Amstetten-Mauer Hospital—built by the Nazis as a death camp in the Second World War—was where the Fritzl family was cared for in the months after the case broke.

"They just seemed so normal," he later told David Jones of London's *Daily Mail*. "The two teenage girls and their younger brother were smartly dressed and really polite, unlike some kids we serve."

During the meal, a jovial Josef Fritzl held court, telling jokes.

"There was lots of laughter from their table," recalled Saham, "particularly when the father cracked a joke."

All three children were top students at their various schools. Alexander, now 10, could always be relied upon to help other students if they struggled in their English and German classes, two subjects in which he excelled. He was an award-winning athlete and a member of the school ice-hockey team. "He has a lot of feeling for the others," said classmate Jelena Krsic "and whenever someone cried, he helped them." But Jelena also remembers Alexander breaking down in tears in front of the other children after once failing in a jumping competition.

On August 23, 2006, Natascha Kampusch escaped, after more than eight years' imprisonment in her underground cellar. Wolfgang Priklopil had allowed his captive, now 18, far more freedom than Josef Fritzl ever gave his. Just before 1:00 p.m., she had been vacuuming his BMW in the garden, when Priklopil received a phone call.

While his back was turned, Natascha, in a desperate dash to freedom, vaulted over several neighbors' fences and ran across gardens, screaming at astonished passers-by to call the police.

But everyone ignored her. Finally, she banged on an elderly lady's kitchen window, shouting, "I am Natascha Kampusch!"

Finally someone called the police, who arrived minutes later, bringing Kampusch to the Deutsch-Wagram police station.

As soon as police identified Kampusch, they launched a manhunt for Priklopil. After a dramatic police chase, he managed to get away in his BMW, heading to Vienna.

A few hours later he committed suicide by jumping in front of an oncoming commuter train outside Vienna's Wien Nord station.

On September 6, two weeks after her escape, Kampusch gave an exclusive interview to the main Austrian TV station ORF, about her eight-year ordeal. It was a huge international story, and the now beautiful and highly photogenic former captive suddenly found herself a genuine Austrian superstar, being compared to Princess Diana.

The interview had one of the biggest television audiences in Austrian history, with an estimated 90 percent of televisions tuned to it.

It can only have given hope to Elisabeth and her children, who reportedly watched it on their cellar television, which was never turned off.

In June 2007, 16-year-old Lisa Fritzl graduated from Kloster's Private School. She attended a big farewell celebration with all her friends, wearing a beautiful party dress her grandfather had bought her for the occasion.

"Lisa looked very pretty in her dress," recalled one former classmate.

All three upstairs children never wanted for anything financially. But that had far more to do with their nurturing grandmother than her husband, who did little except grudgingly pay the bills.

"Rosemarie was a devoted parent," said the classmate. "Josef never came to parent evenings and was never mentioned by her."

Lisa Fritzl was a good-natured teenager, often playing class clown.

"[She] would always make us laugh," recalled the classmate, "and was very popular. She was just a normal, happy kid."

But before saying good-bye to her classmates that June, Lisa had never discussed her future plans.

An enthusiastic member of the social arm of the Amstetten fire brigade, Rosemarie would bring along Monika and Alexander to learn elementary first aid and other survival skills.

She also attended all the brigade's social functions, baking Christmas cookies and cooking large bowls of spaghetti, helped by the children.

"They were both always willing to learn," said brigade member Karl Dallinger. "They were good kids, they seemed to be happy."

That summer, Alfred Dubanovsky had a confrontation with his landlord, and was told to leave.

After twelve years living there, he had noticed how Fritzl avoided trouble with the law at any cost. Once, when police had come over after a problem with a neighbor's apartment, Fritzl had become visibly scared, doing everything he could to settle things, to avoid an escalation.

"I used that when I moved out," said Dubanovsky. "He refused to pay for my new security door. I threatened to sue, he went pale, and as I suspected, the problem was resolved."

Just a few weeks earlier, while chatting with Dubanovsky, Fritzl had made a strange comment that didn't seem important at the time.

"One day this house is going to make history," Fritzl declared, before turning on his heel and walking off.

The now 72-year-old Josef Fritzl was becoming increasingly paranoid. When neighbors wanted to prune a hedge overlooking his garden, the old man lashed out angrily, ordering them to stop.

All the time and energy needed to maintain his two families was tiring him out. He was finding it increasingly difficult to juggle the various parts of his lives, without dropping any.

That long, cold winter, his prisoners in the cellar were constantly sick. Like her mother, Kerstin's teeth were falling out, and all four had suffered flu and acute coughing attacks, as well as circulation and heart problems. At Elisabeth's urging, Fritzl had brought in over-the-counter medicines, easily purchased at a drugstore with no questions asked, but they had not helped.

His cure-all drug of choice had always been aspirin, but it did little to help such serious ailments. Felix and Kerstin were the worst affected, both running high fevers. The 4-year-old boy sometimes shook for hours, while his elder sister had screaming fits.

Josef Fritzl was tiring of all the subterfuge required to feed and clothe his underground family. There was also the question of sex—he was no longer attracted to Elisabeth, with her loss of teeth and snow-white hair, and Kerstin was gravely ill.

So he was now contemplating somehow bringing Elisabeth and the children upstairs, looking for a plausible explanation for their sudden appearance into the world. He had seriously considered the final solution of killing them all. But disposing of Elisabeth and the three children would be far more difficult than throwing the body of a 3-day-old baby into the incinerator.

"I was getting older," he would later explain. "I was finding it harder to move, and I knew that in the future I would no longer be able to care for my second family in the cellar."

By Christmas, Josef Fritzl had come up with a diabolical plan to bring his captive family into the real world. He planned to use his original story of Elisabeth running away to join a cult to account for her sudden reappearance with Kerstin, Stefan and Felix. He would explain their deplorable mental and physical condition by blaming the cult for treating them badly.

So once again he handed Elisabeth a sheet of paper and a pen for another letter. In this one she told her parents she was finally tiring of the religious sect, and wanted to come home. It mentioned Kerstin's medical problems, saying she hoped the whole family would soon be reunited and celebrating birthdays together.

"But it's not possible yet," he dictated. "If all goes well, I hope to be back within six months."

He then mailed the letter from a post office many miles outside Amstetten, timing it to arrive during the Christmas holiday, as a special present for his wife.

CHAPTER 16

Into the Light

At the Fritzl family reunion that Christmas, Josef solemnly announced that he had received a new letter from Elisabeth. She had finally come to her senses, and was now considering leaving the cult to come home with her three children. Over the next few months he spoke of little else, paving the way for their entry into the world.

But at the beginning of April 2008, his carefully laid plans were thrown into disarray when Kerstin became dangerously ill and started having seizures, due to lack of fresh oxygen. Elisabeth gave her aspirin, which was no help whatsoever in fighting the infection.

Kerstin then had a complete mental and physical breakdown, and began tearing out her own hair in clumps. Then, to protest her abysmal living conditions, she ripped off her clothes, throwing them into the toilet to block it up.

Her mother could do little except watch her eldest daughter's condition deteriorate, and try to comfort her between her seizures.

On Wednesday, April 16, Elisabeth's 42nd birthday, her father came into the cellar bearing a present. She then begged him to set Kerstin free, so she could get medical treatment. It was now painfully obvious just how ill the 19-year-old girl was, and Fritzl knew she could no longer survive in the cellar.

Nevertheless, he decided to wait until Rosemarie left on her annual vacation to northern Italy with a friend. He reasoned that this would give him ample time to take her to the hospital and have her treated, before bringing her back into the cellar to stage their return.

The following Friday night, after Rosemarie departed for Italy, Kerstin's condition deteriorated further. She began cramping and having convulsions, biting her lips until they bled. Then she lost consciousness.

Once again, Elisabeth tearfully pleaded with her father to take Kerstin to the hospital and save her life. Finally he agreed, instinctively adapting his plans to suit the emergency situation.

But first he dictated a note for Elisabeth to write, explaining Kerstin's predicament to doctors.

"Please help her," it read. "She has never been in a hospital before."

As he was no longer strong enough to carry Kerstin out of the cellar and upstairs on his own, he asked Elisabeth to help him.

And so, in the early hours of Saturday, April 19, Elisabeth Fritzl finally came back into the light, after spending more than half her life in the underground cellar. It was the first time in twenty-four years that she had seen natural light and breathed fresh air.

But her taste of freedom would be short-lived. For as soon as she helped her father lay Kerstin out on the doorstep, he led her back into the dungeon, slamming the concrete door on her once again.

Once upstairs, Josef Fritzl dialed the emergency services, reporting that he had found an unconscious young woman on his doorstep. Then he peered through a window, observing an ambulance arrive and EMS staff putting Kerstin on a stretcher, before driving off.

Three hours later, he drove to the Mostviertel Amstetten-Maurer state hospital, heading straight for the emergency room. There he demanded to see a doctor immediately, as he had vital information about his recently admitted granddaughter.

He was shown into Dr. Albert Reiter's office, where he handed the head of intensive care a note, saying it was from his daughter Elisabeth, who had left it in his granddaughter's coat pocket, after abandoning her on his doorstep a few hours earlier.

Then he told the doctor about Elisabeth's past with the cult, and how she had already left three of her babies on his doorstep, before Kerstin this morning.

After asking Dr. Reiter to cure his granddaughter as soon as possible and not to go to the police, he walked out.

Later that morning, Josef Fritzl's fears were realized, when a policeman arrived at Ybbsstrasse 40. It was a routine visit, seeking an explanation about Kerstin's condition and her circumstances. But the master manipulator stayed cool, once again recounting his fictitious story about the cult, producing Elisabeth's Christmas letter, and saying that she would soon be home.

After the policeman left, Josef Fritzl could do little but wait.

On Monday, April 21, Fritzl received a telephone call from Dr. Reiter, saying that Kerstin's condition had deteriorated and she was near death. The doctor said he had no idea what was wrong with her, but she had suffered multiple organ failure and had been placed in a medically induced coma. He stressed that there was no time to waste, and they *had* to contact her mother Elisabeth to save her life.

Fritzl curtly replied that he had no idea where his daughter was or what sect she was living with. Then, saying he had to go, he put down the telephone.

After a lifetime of total control, he now felt it all slipping away from him.

The same day, Rosemarie Fritzl sent her family a postcard from Lake Maggiore, completely unaware of what was taking place back in Amstetten.

"Dear family," she wrote.

My holiday has been lovely. Although I'm really busy every day, I fall into bed tired. But I will soon be home, Love, Mama

That night, ORF's evening news broadcast a story on Kerstin, with Dr. Reiter appealing for any information about Elisabeth. After watching the news segment, Fritzl contacted his 69-year-old wife in Italy, saying she had better come home immediately, as Elisabeth had abandoned her sick daughter on their doorstep.

The next day, when reporters knocked on his door for an interview, he lost control. They had been expecting a concerned, cooperative grandfather, but came face-to-face with a furious Josef Fritzl, berating them and cursing out Dr. Reiter for making trouble. Then he threw them off his property, ordering them never to return.

On Wednesday, when police arrived at the house, requesting a DNA sample, Fritzl said he was too busy to provide one, fearful that it would prove that he was Kerstin's father. Over the next two days, Rosemarie—who had now returned home—Lisa, Monika and Alexander all gave DNA samples. But he kept making excuses and postponing it.

Down in the cellar, Elisabeth had spent the week worrying about Kerstin's condition, and comforting Stefan and Felix. Whenever their father visited, they asked for news about Kerstin, but he said little, only that she was recovering.

On Friday morning—six days after Kerstin had been admitted to the hospital—Josef Fritzl telephoned the district governor of Amstetten, Hans-Heinz Lenze, thanking him for the excellent treatment she was receiving. The 64-year-old civil servant oversaw the Amstetten police, the town's hospitals and the social services department, as well as supervising planning permissions for the district. Fritzl impressed the busy district governor with his politeness and good manners.

That night, Elisabeth and the children were in front of the television, watching the ORF evening news. Suddenly, a photograph of a teenage Elisabeth came on the screen, as Dr. Reiter appealed for her to contact the hospital immediately, as they desperately needed Kerstin's medical information to save her life.

"I can't simply look on," Elisabeth saw the emotional doctor tell a reporter. "I am deeply distressed about this case. I have never seen anything like it."

When her father next came into the cellar, Elisabeth confronted him with the news report. She pleaded with him to release her to save Kerstin's life. She promised it would just be "temporarily," and she would return to the cellar once she had visited the hospital.

By Saturday morning, Josef Fritzl had reached a decision. He had no choice but to free Elisabeth and the children if he was to maintain his charade.

But first he made a bargain with Elisabeth, making her swear that in return for all their freedom, she would maintain the illusion that she had been in the fictitious cult for the last twenty-four years. She would also have to coach Stefan and Felix, to back this up. She must also admit to abandoning Lisa, Monika and Alexander on his doorstep and swear never to betray him.

After so long in captivity, and to save Kerstin's life, she had no choice but to agree to his terms.

Later that morning, while Rosemarie and the three upstairs children were out of the house, Josef Fritzl brought Elisabeth, Stefan and Felix out of the cellar and into the daylight.

It had been 8,516 days since he had first lured Elisabeth into the dungeon.

A few hours later, Rosemarie Fritzl and her three grandchildren arrived home to discover three strangers in their living room. Her husband then announced that Elisabeth had finally come home with her two children. Mother and daughter, who now looked more like elderly sisters, fell into each other's arms, bursting into tears. It was the first time they had seen each other in twenty-four years, and they were both overcome with emotion. Stefan and Felix just sat there, too shocked to do anything.

That evening, Josef Fritzl telephoned Dr. Albert Reiter, announcing that Elisabeth had come home. He said he would drive her straight to the hospital to be reunited with Kerstin. Once again he asked the doctor not to alert police, as it would only embarrass Elisabeth and the family.

And then Elisabeth walked out of Ybbsstrasse 40 for the first time in almost a quarter of a century, for the short drive to the hospital.

CHAPTER 17

Freedom

After Elisabeth Fritzl walked into the Mostviertel Amstetten-Mauer state hospital announcing that she was Kerstin's mother and offering her help, she was brought into Dr. Albert Reiter's office. Outside on the hospital grounds her father nervously waited for her in his Mercedes.

"She appeared very strange," the doctor later told *Stern* magazine. "Of course I wanted to ask her where she had been for the last twenty-four years, but that was not my job at this moment."

So Dr. Reiter limited his questioning to Kerstin's illness and how it had started. Elisabeth told him about Kerstin's symptoms, and what little she had been able to do to help her, without mentioning their cellar imprisonment. Then she said she had to go.

As soon as Elisabeth left his office, Dr. Reiter alerted Amstetten police.

A few minutes later, Josef and Elisabeth Fritzl were picked up at the hospital gates and brought to police headquarters, where they were placed in separate rooms for questioning. Detectives were far more concerned with Elisabeth than her father, as they still believed she was a bad mother who had abandoned her children.

"The questioning focused on [her]," said Colonel Franz Polzer, head of the Lower Austrian police criminal investigation unit, who would lead the investigation. "Where she had been and why she had neglected her children."

The "extremely psychologically disturbed," ashen-haired woman refused to speak, just staring blankly at the wall in front of her. But after several hours of gentle coaxing and assurances she would never have to see her father again, and that she and her children would be protected against him, she finally broke down and told her story.

"It was quite late, around midnight," recalled Colonel Polzer, "that she revealed that she hadn't abandoned her children. She had been incarcerated for twenty-four years."

For the next two hours, shocked investigators took notes, as Elisabeth told her incredible story. She spoke very fast, without a break, often taking lengthy pauses to compose herself, trying to summon up the right words.

She told how, from the age of 11, she had been "continuously abused" by her father. He had raped her in the cellar, in his car and during walks in the woods, and she had been too ashamed to tell anyone.

Then as detectives listened in disbelief, Elisabeth recounted how her nightmare had started on August 28, 1984, when her father asked her for help to move a door into the cellar. He had then taken her by surprise, drugging her with ether. Later she had awoken to find herself handcuffed to a post in a dark dungeon.

Then he had brutally raped her again and again, before leaving her "shackled like an animal," until he returned several days later. This time he had attached a thick cable leash around her waist, tethering her to a pole in the middle of the tiny dungeon.

"The only thing I could do," she told the amazed investigators, "was to go to the toilet."

She had tried to fight back, banging on the concrete walls and screaming until she was hoarse. But she had finally given up, realizing it was useless and no one could hear her.

After she stopped fighting him, her father had stopped his savage beatings, although he still demanded sex when he visited the dungeon every two or three days to feed her.

"I faced the choice," she explained, "of either being left to starve or being raped."

Eventually, after nine months in captivity, he had let her off the leash, allowing her to move around the cramped dungeon, warning her that if she ever tried to escape, a deadly gas would be released.

Four years into her imprisonment, she had become pregnant, as he was not using any contraception. Initially she feared he would be furious, thinking he would now have to take her to a hospital to have the baby. But he had only sneered, saying she wouldn't get away so easily. She had miscarried, but soon became pregnant again.

In the weeks leading up to the birth, he had stopped demanding sex. He had brought in a medical book to guide her through childbirth. She would have to deliver the baby on her own, as he wanted no part of it.

Soon after Kerstin was born in 1988, he demanded sex again. And soon she became pregnant, giving birth to Stefan a year later.

Over the next few years, she related, her father had gradually relaxed his strict control, as she had given birth to Lisa and Monika, who he had then snatched away and taken upstairs, after forcing her to write notes explaining their sudden appearance.

Then Elisabeth became highly emotional, telling investigators how she had delivered twins, Alexander and Michael, who had severe respiratory problems. She had nursed Michael for three days without any medicine, before he died in her arms after he had refused to take the baby to the hospital.

Her father had then dumped his tiny body in the incinerator, taking his twin brother Alexander upstairs, nine months later. By this time he had forced Elisabeth to dig a passageway to enlarge the cellar, adding an extra two rooms.

In 2002, after giving birth to Felix, her seventh and last child, her father had stopped demanding sex.

Then she told the stunned investigators how Kerstin's illness had launched the chain of events that led to their freedom that morning. She said her father had acted alone, and her mother had known nothing about her imprisonment.

When Elisabeth finally finished her statement in the early hours of Sunday morning, it filled eight large sheets of notepaper.

"In a mere two hours she gave an account of the twenty-four years she'd spent in the cellar," said District Governor Hans-Heinz Lenze. "Well, it still sends shivers down my spine."

The detectives then turned their attention to Josef Fritzl, waiting in a nearby interview room. At first he refused to discuss the matter, saying he was sorry, and wanted to be left in peace. But eventually he confessed to building the dungeon and then locking up Elisabeth for twenty four years. Although vague on details, he readily admitted incest, maintaining that there was no force involved. He also admitted threatening Elisabeth and the children with poison gas if they ever tried to escape.

He arrogantly insisted he had done it for Elisabeth's own good, to save her from drugs and bad company.

"I locked up Elisabeth," he declared. "She was a difficult child."

When investigators probed further into his incestuous relationship with Elisabeth, producing seven children, Josef Fritzl was unfazed.

"Yes, I did have sex with her," he replied casually. "But I haven't for many months now."

He also said the reason he had taken three of the children upstairs to be brought up by his wife Rosemarie, was that "They were sickly, and cried too much for my liking," and he feared their bawling would attract unwelcome attention.

He was asked what would have happened if he had been taken sick or died during one of his extended vacations to Thailand. Fritzl said he had taken that into account, installing a sophisticated timer device to open the concrete doors and free his hostages after a certain length of time.

He also claimed to have been in the final stages of preparing to release Elisabeth and the three children, as he was finding it harder and harder to keep up the dungeon as he got older.

Finally, he was asked if he now regretted what he had done.

"Why should I be sorry?" he replied. "I always cared for them. I meant it well. I saved Elisabeth from drugs."

Then Josef Fritzl signed a confession and submitted to a DNA test, before being arrested for incest and keeping his children in captivity.

"He has showed no remorse for his victims," said a police investigator who was present. "He is so arrogant that I don't actually think that he thinks that he has done anything wrong."

Late Saturday night, as Josef Fritzl was being interrogated, Chief Inspector Leopold Etz, the head of Lower Austria's murder squad, arrived at Ybbsstrasse 40 to bring Stefan and Felix to the hospital for a medical examination. Apart from Josef Fritzl, Elisabeth and Kerstin, Etz and his officers were the first human beings the two boys had ever seen.

"They both looked terrified and were terribly pale," Etz remembered. "We did not know what to expect, and were very surprised at how well-mannered and educated they were."

It was the first time the boys had been exposed to natural light in their entire lives, and they had trouble adjusting to it. Everything was new. The only idea they had of the world outside the cellar was from years of watching television.

"The real world was completely alien to them," said the chief inspector. "They appeared overawed by the daylight they had never experienced before."

When 5-year-old Felix stepped outside and saw the moon for the first time, he screamed with delight, asking if that was God up there and they were in heaven.

"They were just open-mouthed with awe," said Etz. "And nudging each other and pointing."

Although it was only a short drive to Amstetten police headquarters, to the boys it was *the* biggest adventure of their lives, like going to the moon. They had only seen cars on television shows, and the exhilarating experience of actually riding in one had them both in rapturous excitement.

Felix shrieked with pleasure as the vehicle took off

down the main road, the driver going very slowly, so as not to scare them.

"They were amazed at the speed, and really excited," said Etz. "They had never known anything like it [as] they had only seen cars from the TV."

The two brothers were completely mesmerized by headlights, bracing themselves whenever a car came in the other direction, afraid they would have a head-on collision. And Felix, who was petrified, started to hum a melody to himself for reassurance.

"They were shouting and hiding behind the seats," said Etz. "They had seen none of it before. Everything was new—a maze. In all my years as a policeman I have seen a lot, but I have never seen anything that comes even close to this—the way this family has suffered."

When they reached the hospital, Stefan and Felix were reunited with their mother, who had recently arrived from the police station. Then doctors began examining them all to ascertain their medical and psychological conditions and to decide on the best course of treatment. Doctors also hoped that Elisabeth could provide the key to treating Kerstin, now lying in a medically induced coma a few floors below.

Elisabeth was very weak and traumatized, her twenty-four years underground having taken a terrible toll. She had gone down into the cellar a beautiful teenager, but now reentered the world looking like a haggard old woman.

She was badly malnourished, with prematurely white hair, her deathly pale white skin lined with age. She had lost all her teeth, and her gums were black from disease. Her bones were brittle, due to a lack of sunlight. She also walked with a limp and was hunched over, and her speech had also been affected by her ordeal.

Like their mother, Stefan and Felix both had complex medical problems, with defective immune systems, papery white skin, acute vitamin D deficiency and anemia. Stefan, now a grown-up 18-year-old, had a pronounced stoop and trouble with spatial awareness, having never been able to stand up in the low-ceilinged cellar. He was also found to be suffering from serious motor neuron problems, making walking very difficult. Like his sister Kerstin, he had also lost teeth.

Little Felix was the least unhealthy one, with the best chance of a complete recovery. The boy crawled "monkey-style," darting from one end of the room to the other without warning, but he could also walk upright on his two legs, when he wanted to.

All of their eyes had been affected, and doctors gave them dark protective goggles to wear, until they could adapt to normal light. They were also prescribed the strongest available sun cream, to protect their pale skin from sunlight.

When Rosemarie Fritzl discovered the truth about what her husband had done, she reportedly suffered a nervous breakdown and was hospitalized with severe heart problems. It would be several weeks before she could be interviewed by police, to see if she had known anything about her daughter's abduction.

The next morning, Chief Inspector Etz drove Elisabeth and the two children to the Amstetten-Mauer psychiatric clinic, where they would convalesce.

Ironically, it was the same building the Nazis had used during the war to exterminate hundreds under Adolf Hitler's euthanasia laws. Josef Fritzl had been well-acquainted with it during his formative years.

On the way down to the hospital parking lot, the

boys were taken on an elevator. Little Felix was terrified, grabbing on to his mother, as the floor moved beneath him.

Then coming outside into the bright sunlight, Stefan and Felix were almost blinded, seeing the sun for the first time. They shielded their eyes with their hands, before being told not to look into it directly.

"The sun fascinated [Felix] even more than the moon," said Chief Inspector Etz. "When the sunbeams struck his face, he squealed loudly."

On the drive to the clinic, they passed a cow grazing in a field, and the brothers howled with delight, whispering excitedly to each other. They were also delighted to see a stream, asking what it could possibly be.

But the boys were particularly fascinated by the police officers' cell phones, and when Felix first heard a ring tone, he got very excited.

"It made him curious," said Etz. "He was completely bowled over when one of the policemen spoke into his phone."

Over the next few days, the seasoned homicide chief befriended Felix and Stefan, feeling genuinely moved by their plight. He observed how they had invented their own language to communicate in, mainly consisting of "mumbles and grunts," to supplement the basic German they had picked up from their mother and from watching television.

"When they want to articulate themselves," said Etz, "they do try to speak so that others can understand them. But it's clear it takes them an immense amount of effort to do so."

Later that morning, Amstetten District Governor Hans-Heinz Lenze visited Josef Fritzl in his police cell. He was stunned to realize that this was the same man who had telephoned him two days before to thank him.

"It's unbelievable," said Lenze. "Until the very last minute he was carrying on his double life. The next day I went to see him in jail and was astonished to see it was him, because I hadn't associated him with the name.

"I said, 'It was you, Herr Fritzl—I'm appalled by you. How can anyone do such a thing?'

"To which he replied, 'I'm very, very sorry for my family, but it cannot be undone.'

"I replied, 'Why have you waited over twenty-four years to feel pity for them? How do you think your family will ever overcome this trauma?'

"And he said, 'I do not think it will be in this town, or even with a change of identity, as has been rumored.'

"Those were his last words before I left and the cell doors closed again."

CHAPTER 18

A Reunion

On Sunday morning, Rosemarie Fritzl arrived at the Amstetten-Mauer psychiatric clinic for a family reunion, in a special closed-off area. Even before receiving the results of the DNA tests, psychiatrists had decided to bring the "upstairs" and "downstairs" Fritzl children together as soon as possible, as the first step in the long healing process.

No one was underestimating the problems both sets of children now faced. Some nervously pondered all the suffering endured by the Fritzl family, and whether Elisabeth's two sets of children would shun each other. The human-scale implications of this epic meeting were in completely uncharted territory.

What could 69-year-old Rosemarie Fritzl say to her daughter, who she thought had joined a cult and abandoned three children for her to bring up? How could Alexander greet his brothers Stefan and Felix, who he didn't even know existed before yesterday? Then, on top of that, to discover they had been imprisoned their entire lives in a dungeon by their grandfather, who also happened to be their father?

This was totally off the map, and everyone was concerned about the repercussions. But the most worried of all were the various family members.

"They were all very distressed and extremely worried about meeting each other for the first time," said Amstetten-Mauer clinic director Dr. Berthold Kepplinger. "It was a very emotional scene."

When Rosemarie and Elisabeth saw each other again, they fell into each other's arms.

"I can't believe I'm free," sobbed Elisabeth, when she finally let go of her mother. "Is it really you? I didn't think I would ever see you again."

Then Rosemarie apologized, saying she loved her dearly and they would never be parted again.

"I'm so sorry—I had no idea," she sobbed over and over again.

Then Elisabeth declared she never wanted to see her father's face again, after the unspeakable things he had done to her and her children.

"I can't believe I'm out," she said. "It's all too much for me."

Doctors then brought in Lisa, Monika and Alexander, who Fritzl had snatched away to live upstairs.

"My babies!" cried Elisabeth, as she hugged them and stroked their faces. "You are so beautiful."

Then Stefan and Felix came in to meet their upstairs siblings, and grandmother Rosemarie for the first time. The little boy, who had spent his entire life underground, seemed the "most distressed," clinging to his mother the entire time.

"He would jump and start at the slightest disturbance," said Dr. Kepplinger. "Now that the novelty of being free from the cellar has worn off, he needs some peace. After all, in his whole life he had only seen four other people."

Also present were many of Elisabeth's brothers and sisters, including Harald and Gabrielle, who were joining the rest of the family in therapy.

"None of us can believe how normal Elisabeth seems," Gabrielle, 35, later told the London *Daily Mail*. "She is healthy and very chatty and doing very well."

Gabrielle, who lived just outside Amstetten with her partner, said the family was totally devastated by what their father had done.

"I can't say what the family is going through," she said. "It's more than anyone can believe. We are working together to support Elisabeth. She is overjoyed to see her children . . . and she is spending all the time getting to know them."

Clinic Director Dr. Kepplinger, who witnessed the moving reunion, later described it as "a genuinely happy occasion [without being] forced." And from what he'd seen, he was now convinced Rosemarie Fritzl had known nothing of her daughter's imprisonment.

"It was a very moving meeting between Rosemarie and Elisabeth," said Dr. Kepplinger. "[They] said they loved each other and pledged never to be separated again."

The clinic director said things had gone better than anyone dared hope.

"The reunion went incredibly well," he said. "It was astonishing how easily it happened. They got along very well and it was far more successful than anticipated."

But Dr. Kepplinger was circumspect about the huge differences between the well-cared-for family upstairs, and their siblings downstairs, who had had none of their advantages.

"The children who grew up in the cellar are as you'd expect, considering what they've been through," said Dr. Kepplinger. "They can speak and make themselves understood, but they're far from being in a normal state. We are going very slowly."

* * *

Late Sunday night, police finally entered the cellar at Ybbsstrasse 40, with the help of Josef Fritzl, who had been brought back to reveal the complex electronic codes needed to access the dungeon. The police were highly cautious, fearing the cellar had been booby-trapped with explosives or gas.

Fritzl led them through five different rooms in the cellar, to his workshop. He then pointed out the false shelf, containing paint cans and other containers, behind which lay a 660-pound three-foot-high reinforced concrete door on steel rails. Finally, before being taken away, he revealed the electronic codes that opened it, as well as the ones for the other six, leading to the dungeon.

Chief Inspector Franz Polzer and his team of detectives then entered, negotiating their way along the rat-infested, uneven-floored passageway, unlocking the doors one by one. Finally, they entered the dungeon through a four-foot door, discovering a maze of tiny rooms, connected by narrow stone-lined corridors, just 5 feet, 5 inches tall.

They paused for a couple of minutes, allowing their eyes to adapt to the dingy, almost airless cellar, that had housed Elisabeth Fritzl and her three children for so many years.

Inside they found a well-equipped kitchen and two bedrooms, one with a television and shower, with the children's colorful painted posters adorning the plaster walls. They also discovered a cell padded top to bottom with rubber, coming off one of the rooms.

There was also a small bathroom and toilet, with tiles and wood trim, crudely decorated with starfish and other marine animals, and brightly colored paper stars on all four rotting walls and the ceiling.

"I went to see this dungeon, this prison for myself," said Chief Inspector Polzer. "I went through it and was very glad to be able to leave."

Another detective likened it to a scene from a horror movie.

"There are things that you just don't want to see," he said. "The fewer pictures you have in your head, the better."

A few hours later, as teams of forensic scientists began combing through the cellar and the surrounding grounds for evidence, a calm Josef Fritzl arrived at St. Polten jail, 44 miles east of Amstetten. After being fingerprinted and photographed, he was put under suicide watch.

Late Sunday night, the Lower Austrian police released a statement to the press. It stated that they had found a 42-year-old woman, only referred to as Elisabeth F., who had been missing since August 29, 1984, after an anonymous tip-off. A month after her disappearance, Elisabeth F. had been forced by her father to write a letter to her parents asking them not to search for her. The statement went on to outline how Josef F. and his wife Rosemarie had alerted authorities, after finding three babies left outside their home in 1993, 1994 and 1997, each accompanied by a note from the mother.

The statement said police had brought Elisabeth and her father to police headquarters on Saturday night. During questioning, Elisabeth had revealed that her father had first begun molesting her when she was 11. Then, in August 1984, he'd sedated and handcuffed her, locking her into the cellar for the next twenty-four years.

During her incarceration, said the statement, she had given birth to seven of his children, one dying soon after being born. Three of the younger children had been found on his doorstep, along with letters from his kidnapped daughter Elisabeth. So they were brought up by Josef and his wife Rosemarie as adopted or foster children.

As Austrian reporters converged on Ybbsstrasse 40, Chief Inspector Polzer gave an impromptu press conference.

"It is one of *the* most remarkable criminal cases in Austria," stated the white-haired veteran policeman.

He then outlined the chronology of events leading to the discovery of the cellar, emphasizing that Rosemarie Fritzl had not known about her daughter's imprisonment, believing that Elisabeth had run away and joined a cult.

"The father seems to be very authoritarian," he told TV news reporters, "and decided what happened and what was supposed to happen in the family—and today we know why he very closely guarded the basement."

He said police were awaiting the results of DNA tests, to definitely determine the paternity of Elisabeth's six surviving children.

"They all apparently share the same father," he said.

In the days to come, the incredible story—by far eclipsing the Natascha Kampusch kidnapping—would capture the imagination of the world and plunge Austria into a national scandal.

When Amstetten residents awoke the next morning, learning the full horror of the crime Josef Fritzl had perpetrated in their midst, there was stunned disbelief. Ybbsstrasse was a main shopping street, and every one of the town's 23,000 residents had walked past his house at one time or another.

And while Elisabeth and the children had been held

captive, more than one hundred tenants had lived there, just a few feet over the cellar dungeon. Finally all the late-night banging and other strange occurrences started making sense. Within hours of the story breaking, someone placed a sign outside the house, reading, "Why did nobody notice?"

The Austrian press immediately dubbed Josef Fritzl "Das Inzest-Monster," branding his actions "The Worst Crime in History." Many were now looking back at Austria's role in the Second World War, asking if this was just the latest and worst example yet of a national malaise.

Now the troubled country, only just coming to terms with the horrific eight-year kidnapping of Natascha Kampusch, had a new and far lower benchmark for depravity.

"The community of Amstetten should drown in shame," declared a Monday morning editorial in the *Osterreich*. "The neighbors are turning a blind eye."

In the wake of the story, onlookers milled around the drab three-story Fritzl house, watching the forensic teams of investigators go in and out.

"I only have a small pension," Gertrude Baumgarten, who once worked with Fritzl, told CNN, "but I would spend my money to see him hang on a rope."

She described him as "arrogant" and someone she deliberately avoided, saying she felt sorry for his wife, who had often spoken of Elisabeth running away.

Like many in Amstetten, Herbert Schneider had considered Josef Fritzl to be the soul of respectability, regularly seeing him breezing around town in his Mercedes-Benz.

"He did not seem to have much to do with many people here," Schneider recalled. "But he was always very friendly."

Erika Manhalter, who grew up near Josef Fritzl's house, remembered him as aloof, never getting close to anyone.

"It certainly seemed as if they were a perfect family unit," she said. "It just goes to show you cannot really ever see what is happening behind closed doors. I am truly shocked."

And Gunther Pramreiter, who owned the bakery next door to the Fritzls' house, said the old couple or their adopted grandchildren came in every day to buy bread.

"You're amazed that something like this can happen in your neighborhood," he said.

When Josef Fritzl's best friend Paul Hoerer, saw Fritzl's mugshot, accompanying news reports of his arrest, he was speechless.

"I thought there must be some mistake," he said. "A mix-up."

Hoerer and his girlfriend Andrea Schmitt, who had often vacationed with Fritzl, last visiting his home three years earlier, could not believe it possible.

"Now I think of the dungeon down there," he said. "I feel sick. I am ashamed to be linked to him."

The only member of the Fritzl family willing to give an interview was Jurgen Helm, who was married to Elisabeth's younger sister Gabrielle. He told the *Austrian Times* that he and his wife had once spent three years living at Ybbsstrasse 40, even going down into the cellar on several occasions.

"I had no idea that a few meters away, this family [was] living," he said.

As hundreds of reporters converged on Amstetten from all over the world, all the grown-up Fritzl children went into hiding. Hours after her husband's brief interview, Gabrielle Helm had placed a sign on her chalet-style home just outside Amstetten, reading, "Reporters not welcome." And in the coming weeks, her brothers and sisters refused to talk to the press during their frequent trips to the Amstetten-Mauer psychiatric hospital for counseling.

Elisabeth's older brother Harald, 44, who she had always been closest to growing up, would be particularly important in her recovery. He and their sister Doris would also help detectives build a case against their father.

Later, when reporters tracked Harald Fritzl down to a little cottage in Mitterkirchen im Machland, fifteen miles from Amstetten near the River Danube, his wife came out, screaming, "Leave us alone!"

On Monday afternoon, police released color photographs of the cellar, refusing reporters' requests for pictures of the bedrooms and rubber-padded cell reportedly used by Fritzl to rape his daughter.

At a press conference held in a local hotel, Chief Inspector Franz Polzer, District Governor Hans-Heinz Lenze and Mauer clinic director Dr. Berthold Kepplinger all sat at a table, briefing the media.

"He was a man of stature," declared Polzer, holding up a large photograph of Josef Fritzl, taken soon after his arrest. "He led a double life with a family of seven children, with his wife, and a second family of seven children with his daughter. If you look at him today, you would hardly believe he was capable of doing these things."

Polzer said his men were searching several other properties Fritzl owned around Amstetten, although he doubted they would find any further dungeons, as this one must have occupied most of his time.

"We have not found a further hiding place or a dungeon," he said. "It's quite logical that Mr. Josef Fritzl was very busy looking after his two families—the family which lived in the house upstairs, and the one he had in the dungeon."

Dr. Kepplinger then addressed the press, saying that Elisabeth's six children were now doing "quite well" at his clinic.

"There's a team of professionals, consisting of a psychiatrist, neurologist, speech therapist and other experts looking after them," he said.

But when a reporter asked for details of the family's daily routine, Chief Inspector Polzer refused to discuss it.

"These regrettable people," he said, "deserve a right to privacy about the intimate details of their life."

The questions then turned to Rosemarie Fritzl, and whether she had helped her husband.

"You have to imagine this woman's world fell apart," said District Governor Lenze, visibly shocked by what had happened.

Reporters then asked how Fritzl could have gotten away with it for so long, after at least twenty visits from social services over the years.

Lenze, in charge of Amstetten social services for the last fifteen years, defended the authorities. He pointed out that if Fritzl had been able to fool his wife for so long, and they lived in the same house, what chance did anyone else have?

"The criminal is always one step ahead of the police," he explained. "If we had sensed something, we would have acted."

Late Monday night, the English tabloid newspapers printed a series of color photographs, showing Josef Fritzl enjoying himself on a beach in Thailand, more than five thousand miles away from his captives. The photographs, taken in January 1998 during one of his sex vacations to Pattaya, came from a video that his best friend Paul Hoerer had shot on the trip. It showed a grinning Fritzl in skimpy Speedos, enjoying a beach massage, sunbathing and shopping in a local bazaar.

Hoerer told reporters how he had become suspicious after he and his girlfriend Andrea Schmitt had once spotted him buying some frilly underwear, far too small for his wife Rosemarie. He said Fritzl had been "really annoyed" when he realized he'd been caught, finally admitting to having a girlfriend, and making him promise to keep it a secret.

He also revealed that Fritzl would disappear late at night, to indulge in Pattaya's infamous sex industry.

"Fritzl had other interests," said Rainer Wieczorak, 62, who accompanied them on the 1998 trip. "He had another agenda."

Hoerer said he had visited the Fritzl home as recently as 2005, and before she was imprisoned, he remembered Elisabeth well as a "withdrawn and shy" child. He said it was obvious that her father did not like her as much as his other children, as he beat her for the smallest thing.

Then, in 1984, Fritzl had told him that Elisabeth had run away and joined a sect. Over the years he remembered how upset Rosemarie would become if her missing daughter was ever brought up in conversation.

"She would leave the table," he said. "But I never saw her cry."

The Fritzl house soon became a ghoulish tourist attraction, drawing hundreds of people who stood staring at it. One of Monika Fritzl's teachers organized a special school trip to view it, so her classmates could have a better idea of what their friend was going through.

"The children are desperate to see it for themselves," said the teacher, refusing to give her name. "There's no point keeping it from them, that will only make it worse, and they'll find out anyway, because it's all anyone's talking about."

CHAPTER 19

"It's Beyond Comprehension"

On Tuesday morning, as doctors battled to save Kerstin Fritzl's life, her father briefly appeared before a judge in St. Polten, the provincial capital of Lower Austria. He was remanded for fourteen-day pre-trial detention, while police continued their investigation. On the way back to jail, he was photographed shielding his face in the back of a police car.

"He was completely calm," prosecutor Gerhard Sedlacek later told reporters. "Completely without emotion."

As each hour brought shocking new details of Josef Fritzl's crimes, the case took center stage in Austrian politics. Just a month away from Austria hosting the much-anticipated European Cup, Interior Minister Günther Platter called for calm, dispatching a team of officials to Amstetten for an official investigation.

"We're being faced with an unfathomable crime," he declared. "This case is one of incomprehensible brutality and horror—the most shattering and serious case of its kind that has ever come to light in Austria."

That morning an Austrian newspaper reported that Josef Fritzl had a previous rape conviction, and had served jail time. The London *Times* quoted a representative of the Amstetten building company Zehetner, which had employed Fritzl in 1969, admitting he was hired with the knowledge that he had been convicted of rape and had served jail time. Another ex-colleague said that in the early 1970s, it was well known in Amstetten that Fritzl was a convicted rapist.

"I can neither confirm nor deny it," said Inspector Polzer defensively, citing Austria's overly lenient privacy laws, erasing criminal records after a fifteen-year period.

On Tuesday afternoon, Chief Inspector Franz Polzer called another press conference, announcing that DNA tests had confirmed Josef Fritzl fathered all his daughter Elisabeth's children. They also proved that no other males had been inside the cellar, ruling out an accomplice.

"We have the results of the DNA," said Polzer. "Josef Fritzl is the true father of these seven children of his own daughter."

Polzer said police were now considering charging Fritzl with "murder through failure to act," as he had admitted throwing the body of his baby son Michael into an incinerator.

"You can be sure this man left nothing undone," said Polzer, "in order to deceive the family, his wife, the relatives, the children and everybody around him. In twenty-four years we have never seen anything like it. It's beyond comprehension."

The inspector said Fritzl had initially designed the prison to fulfill Elisabeth's basic needs, gradually enlarging it as her children were born.

"He had a very high sex drive and libido," explained Polzer, adding that this in itself was not enough to explain his depravity. "He was driven somehow to this behavior, but we don't know why or how. He hasn't given a motive."

The inspector emphasized that the investigation was still in its infancy, and there was much work to do.

"We have been working on this case for about fifty hours now," he said. "We now have to unravel what happened in the past twenty-four years. We have to find out what life was like in this dungeon, in this prison. We have to find how the births came about. Are there people that helped out, perhaps? Are there situations which will be important later on when the judge comes to decide how long this accused man should go to prison?"

Just hours after police denied knowledge of Josef Fritzl's rape conviction, his sister-in-law, Christine R., confirmed it in a BBC interview. Refusing to disclose her last name, she said that after he'd served 18 months' jail time, her sister had only decided to stay with him to keep her family of four children together.

"I think it changed their relationship," she said. "A woman in such a situation would have been utterly broken and shocked when something like this happened."

She attacked the Austrian legal system, for purging criminal offenses from the record books after fifteen years, allowing him to get away with his crimes.

"Sexual offenses should never be deleted from criminal records," she declared. "If they had known, perhaps then the authorities would have kept a better eye on him."

Her older sister, she said, had known nothing about Elisabeth's imprisonment. Josef had often spent "whole nights" down in the cellar, working on technical plans for an unspecified machine, and could never be disturbed.

"I always hated him," Christine declared. "If Josef

was still free, I would never have dared to give this interview."

She said Rosemarie was "dominated and constantly belittled in public" by Fritzl, and not even allowed to bring him a cup of coffee while he was down there.

For the first time, Christine revealed Fritzl's violent childhood under the Nazi Third Reich. She said that to instill discipline, his mother had used her fists to beat him "black and blue" every day, something he would later replicate with his children.

He was a ruthless tyrant, she said, treating his children as army privates, constantly punishing them for the smallest infringement of his rules.

"The only chance the children had to escape this atmosphere was by marrying," she said. "And all of them did that as soon as they were old enough."

She said her sister was "shattered" when she learned what Josef had done.

"I can say with one hundred percent certainty that she knew nothing," said Christine. "Otherwise she would have spoken with our siblings about it. She was so shocked and never believed him capable of it."

And although she had not spoken to Rosemarie since the discovery of the cellar, Christine claimed to have been kept up-to-date with the family's progress in the Amstetten-Mauer clinic.

"The children are in half-decent shape physically," she said. "But my sister is doing very badly and Elisabeth is not in the best shape. I know my sister, and when something is wrong with her children, the world collapses. For sure the world has collapsed for her."

On Tuesday evening, staff at the Amstetten-Mauer clinic threw a party to celebrate Alexander Fritzl's twelfth birthday. He received presents of a Lego set and stuffed animals, as well as a birthday cake with twelve candles, blowing them out to the rousing cheers of his brothers and sisters.

Then a prayer was said for Kerstin, lying in a coma a few miles across Amstetten, while undergoing dialysis and on a respirator.

It was the first real family occasion for the newly reunited Fritzl family, marking an important landmark in their long road to recovery.

"The family is doing well under the circumstances," said clinic director Dr. Kepplinger. "They are talking a lot with each other."

He said the family now resided in a closed-off section of the clinic. The windows had been darkened to help Elisabeth, Stefan and Felix adapt to the light, as well as preventing any photographs being taken of them from the outside.

Doctors had also installed a cargo container, replicating a smaller version of the dungeon, where the family could retreat, if the outside world became too much. Stefan had been given a goldfish aquarium, like the one Fritzl had installed inside the dungeon. Some of their treasured personal items had been brought to the clinic, to help the former captives feel more comfortable.

Dr. Kepplinger said that Elisabeth was now getting along "very well" with Rosemarie, and both sets of children were getting to know each other. But Felix, who would celebrate his sixth birthday with his own cake two days later, was still too scared to leave his mother's side, refusing to let go of his favorite teddy bear, which his father had once given him as a present.

"We are pleased with their progress," said Dr. Kepplinger. "The family seems to feel okay here, and that is vital before any attempt is made to slowly ease them back into normal life. What the family really need[s] right now is time."

As the Fritzl family celebrated Alexander's birthday, more than four hundred people gathered for a candle-light vigil for them in Amstetten town square.

"We want to show that this is not a town of crimi-nals," Mayor Herbert Katzengruber told the crowd, "and to counteract the impression of Amstetten which has arisen. These have been awful and sad days. I'm appalled and saddened that such a thing could happen in my hometown."

The event had been organized by a newly founded Amstetten citizens' initiative group, showing solidarity for Elisabeth and the children.

After the vigil, there was a procession to Ybbsstrasse 40, where supporters solemnly laid flowers outside the Fritzl house.

"We have been surrounded by shock, sadness, an-ger, perhaps even hate in the last few days," said Am-stetten priest Peter Bosendorfer. "We were forced to recognize that there is something in our town that we cannot comprehend."

CHAPTER 20

"Hey, Satan, Come Out and Play!"

On Wednesday, April 30, Austrian Chancellor Alfred Gusenbauer announced a major public relations campaign to restore Austria's good image in the wake of the Josef Fritzl scandal. He wanted to send out a global message that Austria was not the "land of the dungeons," and Fritzl was not representative of its people.

"We won't allow a whole country to be held hostage by one man," he declared. "It is not Austria that is the perpetrator. This is an unfathomable criminal case, but also an isolated one."

With just a month before Austria and Switzerland would jointly host Euro 2008, the government hired an international public relations company, specializing in crisis management, to use "all technical and professional means" to "rectify" Austria's tarnished image. Chancellor Gusenbauer pledged that during the two-week soccer tournament, when the eyes of the world would be on Austria, the country would be presented in its true light: a nation of the highest social standards and quality of life.

But the public relations strategy was not well received by many, who felt it insensitive and insulting to Elisabeth Fritzl and her children.

"It would make sense to start looking for answers, many of which are slumbering within ourselves," cautioned an editorial in the *Kurier* newspaper, "instead of reacting in a patriotic knee-jerk way."

That night, Natascha Kampusch appeared on the British current affairs show *Newsnight*, describing the Fritzl tragedy as a direct result of the Third Reich sexism.

"At the time of National Socialism," she said, "the suppression of women was propagated, and authoritarian education was very important. It's a ramification of the Second World War."

She said she had been closely following the Fritzl story, fully identifying with it after her own eight-year hostage ordeal. She announced a $37,000 donation to the family, calling for others to follow her example.

"Little by little, I realized there were parallels to my own fate," she explained. "So then the whole story affected me even more. [I wish] the family the best of luck and hope that they will pull through, and I think that at least the youngest one will succeed."

Soon afterwards a special fund was set up to raise money for the Fritzl family—for it now appeared that Josef Fritzl was almost $3 million in debt, and there would be no money to cover the family's medical and psychological care and education, expected to cost at least $1.4 million and take up to eight years.

Many Austrian newspapers, television stations and celebrities appealed for funds to help the family.

"We know that there will be no compensation coming from Josef Fritzl, whose property speculation has left him almost bankrupt," wrote the *Osterreich* in an editorial. "It is not enough to have vague promises from politicians. We need to act."

* * *

While Austria still reverberated from the shock waves of his depravity, Josef Fritzl appeared strangely unaffected by it all. He was now sharing a tiny cell at St. Polten prison with a 36-year-old inmate accused of attempted murder, spending much of his time reading about himself in newspapers and watching the non-stop television coverage.

"He wants to see every word written about him and watch every TV report," said a prison source. "It's like a game to him."

Ironically, his ten-foot-high prison cell was a palace compared to the dungeon where he had imprisoned Elisabeth and the children. It had a television, radio and stereo system, with a constant supply of newspapers and magazines. There was a comfortable bed with clean sheets, a bedside lamp, a table with two chairs and even a potted plant by the large window.

He ate three square meals a day, designed by prison nutritionists, with fresh fruit and vegetables.

All of his fellow inmates knew about the case, and he now feared for his life, as sexual offenders were hated on the inside. On arrival, he had taken full advantage of the daily one-hour exercise period to walk around the sunny yard, but he soon stopped after receiving threats from other inmates. Every night they would bang on his cell wall and taunt him, screaming, "Hey, Satan, come on out and play—we are going to get you!"

"Fritzl is terrified someone will kill him," said a prison warden. "The other prisoners call him 'Satan,' and the only reason he's sharing a cell is so his roommate can report on him and check that he doesn't try to commit suicide."

The word soon spread through the jail grapevine

that Fritzl was "the worst kind of scum that needed to be dealt with." There was a price on his head, to go to the first inmate to attack or kill him.

Josef Fritzl had always enjoyed watching true crime documentaries on television, and now that he needed the services of a lawyer, he knew exactly where to go.

"He selected me," said the 60-year-old high-profile Vienna attorney Rudolf Mayer, who had defended some of Austria's most notorious criminals. "He had seen me on television, and of course I agreed right away."

The one-time ballet dancer, whose Vienna law office is a few blocks away from where Sigmund Freud once lived, views himself as a therapist/lawyer. One of his most infamous previous cases had been the Austrian Black Widow Elfriede Blauensteiner, believed to have murdered at least seven elderly men, including her second husband, Rudolf. The glamorous grandmother in her sixties patronized the casinos of Vienna, dressing in expensive fur coats and dazzling jewelry.

She preyed on lonely, rich old men, placing advertisements in lonely-hearts columns, describing herself as a "homely housewife and nurse," seeking love and romance.

After persuading her unfortunate victims to alter their wills in her favor, she slowly poisoned them with the diabetic drug Euglucon. Then, to celebrate, she would hit the casinos, gambling away her inheritances on the roulette tables.

After successfully killing four men in this manner, Blauensteiner slipped up trying to poison an elderly man named Alois Pichler, to inherit his million-dollar home. When he refused to change his will, she forged one. Then she left him naked in an ice bath in a locked room with the windows open in the dead of winter, until he froze to death.

A relative later became suspicious, and called the police. When she was arrested in January 1996, Blauensteiner eventually confessed to four murders. In 1997, the 64-year-old grandmother was sentenced to life imprisonment for murder and fraud. In 2001, Mayer unsuccessfully represented her in a second trial, after two more of her suspected victims were exhumed, testing positive for Euglucon.

In November 2003, at the age of 72, she died in prison of a brain tumor, while writing her memoirs.

Making himself immediately available to the press, Mayer said he was not shocked by what Josef Fritzl had done, although agreeing that his defense would be a tremendous challenge. But first he would have to alter the present highly negative public perception of his client.

"Josef Fritzl is being portrayed as a horrific monster and sexual tyrant," he explained. "My job is to show him as a human being."

Later he would describe their first jailhouse meeting as a bonding experience, saying his client had absolutely no "negative aura," like other car thieves and criminals he'd represented.

After three decades at the bar, he had learned to go by his "gut instincts."

"The first thirty seconds of a meeting is crucial for establishing psychological contact," explained Mayer. "I believe . . . I succeeded in bonding with Mr. Fritzl. As I first saw him, the Latin term 'paterfamilias' came to mind. It was used to describe the absolute head of the family—caring, but strict . . . a family man with good intentions."

"I am sure of one thing—that there is an explanation for every deed, every criminal act," he said.

At their next meeting, which lasted two hours, Mayer encouraged his new client to discuss his life, giving his version of events.

"[I wanted to know:] Who is Josef Fritzl?" he said. "Why is he the way he is? I just let him talk, and I listened to him," said the defender.

At the end of the meeting, he advised his client not to cooperate any further with investigators.

"He needs a rest," said Mayer. "We will see if he speaks later."

On Wednesday morning, police appealed to every tenant who had ever lived at Ybbsstrasse 40 to come forward and be interviewed.

"In the past twenty-four years, around one hundred people have lived in the house," said Chief Inspector Polzer. "We want to talk to all of them—possibly one of them observed something that at the time didn't seem so important, but could be of relevance, knowing what we do today."

There were now more than thirty detectives and three hundred uniformed officers working around the clock on the Fritzl case, from every conceivable angle. Four-man teams of forensic experts were combing through the house and the cellar. But it was so damp and badly ventilated, they could only work down there for an hour at a time, leading to speculation that Elisabeth and the children must have spent almost all their time either sitting or lying down.

"[It's] overwhelming and oppressive for investigators," said Chief Inspector Polzer. "There is just not enough air to breathe. The investigators keep having to take breaks. We're trying to get as much done as possible, but are having to work out how to do something about air circulation. It is very difficult."

It had been four days since investigators, many of whom would later receive trauma counseling, first entered the cellar, but they were still baffled at its complexity, and much of it was still unmapped.

"There are still areas that we haven't found inside the dungeon," explained Polzer. "I expect it to be at least two weeks before we have answered all the questions we need to know."

Polzer said some parts of the dungeon appeared to be still under construction, leading him to suspect that Fritzl may have been planning further expansions.

"Nobody except Fritzl knew about these spaces," he said. "And we cannot rule out that there are more doors that we have yet to discover. But we simply don't know what his intentions were," said Polzer. "He is no longer cooperating with us, which makes it hard."

Police technicians were also investigating Fritzl's threats of running pipelines into the cellar, to release deadly gas if his captives ever tried to escape.

"He has said during his questioning," said a police spokesman, "that he threatened the children held in the cellar with gas, if anything ever happened. We are checking to see if it is true, or it was simply a threat."

Every night, under cover of darkness, an ambulance drove out of the gates of the stately Amstetten-Mauer psychiatric clinic, past the scores of reporters camped outside. Inside was Elisabeth Fritzl in a nurse's uniform, now well enough to make secret daily visits to the bedside of her daughter Kerstin in the Amstetten hospital.

The 19-year-old girl was still in a deep coma, while

doctors fought to keep her alive, as her kidneys and other organs started shutting down.

"She [is] in a coma between life and death," said Father Franz Halbartschlager, who'd performed the last rites on her soon after she was admitted. "I prayed for her."

Dr. Albert Reiter, who had been treating Kerstin for the last two weeks, said she was in critical condition on life support, and would be kept in a coma indefinitely.

"Our patient is in a severely life-threatening condition, which resulted from a lack of oxygen," he explained. "In addition to twenty years underground, twenty years with no sunlight, twenty years of psychological stress, come other factors like infection."

The rest of Elisabeth's children and her mother Rosemarie were all undergoing intense psychiatric treatment at the Mauer clinic, while getting to know each other with role-playing and other techniques.

"The nice thing is they have started having a little day-to-day life together," said Dr. Kepplinger. "The mother and the grandmother are making breakfast. The children are making their beds. The three from the cellar are enjoying the fresh air and balanced food, and their skin color is slowly changing."

Elisabeth and her downstairs children were now being kept in a low-lit "treatment container," inside a well-guarded 860-square-foot area of the hospital that could be locked from the inside. But psychiatric experts predicted it would take years before the downstairs children could be fully rehabilitated and introduced to the world outside.

"They can be themselves here, undisturbed by anyone," said Dr. Kepplinger. "The kids are playing, jumping about, moving around as they wish. They've got their toys with them, and there are people there for them around the clock. Physically, they are in good condition, and they love the clinic food."

Stefan and Felix now spent hours in the dark treatment container, where they felt safe. The little boy would often crawl in there at night, humming a lullaby his mother had taught him.

Both boys suffered severe nightmares, when they had to be comforted by their mother. But this presented doctors with a problem: part of their treatment was to separate them from Elisabeth, giving them the independence they would need to survive in the outside world.

All their therapists and doctors agreed it would be a long road to their recovery.

Forensic psychiatrist Keith Ablow, M.D., believes that Elisabeth and her children can heal their deep wounds with the right treatment.

"The key is going to be healing professionals to form bonds with each of these individuals," he said. "That's true whether they be psychiatrists, psychologists, pastoral counselors or psychiatric social workers. The goal is for each of them to feel free to slowly build up trust, telling his or her story with all of its darkness. There is tremendous power in human empathy, and when two people connect in a meeting of heart and soul, it can do wonders for the mind."

Josef Fritzl's upstairs and downstairs families were worlds apart, presenting doctors with many complicated problems in treatment.

"In the dungeon, time must have passed very slowly," explained Dr. Kepplinger. "This slow-moving time is something we want to maintain in the clinic."

While Elisabeth, Stefan and Felix had a naturally slow rhythm of life, Lisa, Monika and Alexander desperately wanted to return to school and see their friends again. But the media interest in the family was so intense, none of the children could leave.

"It's a very frustrating situation," said Klaus Schwertner, a Mauer clinic spokesman. "They will probably be here for months."

Their classmates and teachers also missed them, while attempting to come to terms with what had happened.

"How could a father do such a thing?" asked Alexander's 12-year-old school friend Jelena Krsic, describing him as a "A" student in Mathematics, English and German.

Jelena said everyone at the school was devastated, especially the teachers, several of whom wept when they learned what had happened.

"[Alexander] has a lot of feeling for others," said Jelena, "and whenever someone cried, he helped them. Without him, recess is really boring."

CHAPTER 21

"The Devil Himself"

On Thursday, May 1, a local Linz newspaper printed a dramatic interview with the nurse Josef Fritzl had been convicted of raping at knifepoint forty-one years earlier. Identified only as Frau M., the woman, now 65, had seen a news report, recognizing him instantly after so many years.

"I saw his photograph on television and I knew it was him by his eyes," she said. "I could hardly sleep."

She described in vivid detail how the then–father-of-four had crawled into her ground-floor bedroom through a window, while her husband was out working. She had woken up to find him holding a kitchen knife to her neck, threatening to kill her if she screamed.

Frau M., who was a young mother at the time, said that Fritzl, then working for a Linz steel company, was a well-known Peeping Tom, who used to bicycle around the streets late at night, spying on women.

Later that day, a local Austrian newspaper announced it had unearthed old 1967 police records proving that Josef Fritzl was a known sex offender. The files, gathering dust in a basement for nearly four decades, contained his conviction for Frau M.'s rape, for which he'd served 18 months in jail, as well as an earlier one for attempted rape and an arrest for indecent exposure.

A few days later, long-retired Linz Police Chief Gerhard Marwan, 77, told reporters how he had caught Fritzl after the vicious rape.

"We traced him by a print from his palm at the scene," said Marwan. "And he was identified by the victim, a nurse, as well as by a twenty-one-year-old woman, who was attacked in Ebelsbergerwald woods, but managed to escape. As early as 1959, we recorded Fritzl as an exhibitionist."

Red-faced Amstetten police, who had earlier claimed Fritzl did not have a criminal past, confirmed that Linz police had unearthed his rape files, which would be studied at the earliest opportunity.

"We must examine them carefully," said a spokesman for the St. Polten prosecutor's office. "They obviously have great relevance for the case."

On the heels of this shocking revelation, Austrian police announced they now wanted to question Josef Fritzl about the November 1986 unsolved sex murder of 17-year-old Martina Posch, whose naked body had been found close to the boarding house at Lake Mondsee, which Fritzl owned at the time.

Calling it a "routine measure," Police Chief Alois Lissl said that Martina, who had been savagely raped, bore a striking resemblance to Elisabeth, who'd already been down in the cellar two years at the time of the murder.

Now investigators planned to search Ybbsstrasse 40, looking for Martina's clothes and personal possessions, including a pair of black leather boots, a blue jacket and a gray purse that were missing.

"The perpetrator could have kept these items as a kind of trophy," said Chief Lissl. "What really stands out is that Martina looks similar to Elisabeth."

The police chief ultimately admitted that there was

no sign of a "concrete link" to Fritzl, who would nevertheless be asked to account for his movements around the time of the murder.

Over the next few weeks, Austrian police would take a further look at more than 700 unsolved sexual assault and missing persons cases, to see if Josef Fritzl had been involved.

But his defense attorney, Rudolf Mayer, had now instructed his new client to exercise his rights and keep quiet.

"From now on he is not speaking to the police," Mayer told reporters. "He will not say a single word."

He said that as Fritzl faced a possible 15-year sentence for rape, as well as 20 years for the "murder through neglect" of Michael, he might use an insanity defense.

"This case requires a thorough psychiatric and psychological examination," said Mayer. "We need to establish if he can be considered responsible for his actions."

On Friday morning, Amstetten hospital doctors announced that Kerstin's condition had deteriorated, and she was not expected to survive.

"She is suffering from multiple organ failure," said a hospital spokesman. "That means her chances of survival are very low."

St. Polten prosecutors said they would examine the possibility of charging Josef Fritz with murder if his daughter died through his negligence.

The same morning a story appeared in the Austrian Press that Fritzl had left Elisabeth alone for three days, after giving birth to her twins Alexander and Michael. It was only after the baby had died that he had come into the cellar and coldly thrown the body into the incinerator.

"We thought we were dealing with a monster," a police officer told *The Sun*. "But this man is the devil himself. We think he went off sex with Elisabeth when she was heavily pregnant, and left her to have her babies underground. The more we learn about him, the more his actions defy belief. He is morally sub-human."

In another shocking revelation that day, the German magazine *Der Spiegel* claimed it had received information that Fritzl had repeatedly raped Elisabeth in front of Kerstin and Stefan. Elisabeth had told investigators she had spent the first nine years of her incarceration in the one-room dungeon, until the cellar had been enlarged. Therefore, her children must have witnessed their father committing incestuous rape on numerous occasions.

Defender Rudolf Mayer said his client was most upset about the allegations being made against him. He was especially angry that police had accused him of murdering baby Michael by neglect, and for that reason, had stopped cooperating with the investigation.

Mayer accused prosecutors of trying to put his client behind bars for the rest of his life, even though 15 years was the maximum term for murder in Austria.

"My client has admitted Elisabeth had the twins on her own in the cellar," said Mayer. "And that he did not see her until three days after the birth. He told me that when he found one of the babies was dead, he put its body in the furnace."

Mayer said his client was "emotionally destroyed," and had no regrets about anything he had done.

"He thought he was protecting his family," said the lawyer, "and said that was his job as the patriarch."

The following day, Mayer told the *Austrian Times* that he had received several death threats and sack-loads of hate mail since becoming Fritzl's defense attorney.

One letter threatened to come to his office and execute him during Euro 2008.

But he said he would not be intimidated, having received similar threats when he defended "Black Widow" Elfriede Blauensteiner.

"I am getting letters saying that I should be locked up with Fritzl," he complained. "But I am not representing a monster; I am representing a human being."

Mayer had no plans to hire a bodyguard, saying he was "an enthusiastic" amateur boxer, who could look after himself.

"I will not be swayed by a lynch justice mentality," he declared. "Every accused person has the right to a defense. I see the good in my clients and I want to understand them. Perhaps that's why some people hate me."

Over the next few days, several of Josef Fritzl's acquaintances revealed that there had been clues about what was happening in the cellar, now regretting having never spoken up at the time.

Alfred Dubanovsky, who had lived above the dungeon for twelve years, broke down in tears during a television interview, recalling how Fritzl had once told him the house would go down in history.

"I can't stop thinking about it," sobbed the 42-year-old gas-pump attendant. "There were so many clues. The noises at night, the amount of food he used to load into a wheelbarrow and push to the cellar. His wife must have noticed that."

Dubanovsky revealed that he had once seen another man go into the cellar, saying he believed it was a plumber helping Fritzl install a toilet.

"I met a common friend of mine and Elisabeth," said former tenant Josef Leitner, who gave several television interviews, "and told her I was living at Fritzl's house. She said, 'Don't you know who he is?' I said I got along with him and she said, 'He raped Sissy, his daughter.'"

Leitner said he thought the police knew about it, otherwise he would have reported it. He also recalled another tenant telling him about the 1967 rape and suspected arson, showing him newspaper cuttings to prove it.

In hindsight, said the Amstetten waiter, there were many strange goings-on in the house that should have raised suspicions. Every month he would receive huge electricity bills, although he was working construction at the time and was seldom there. Then there was the food, mysteriously disappearing from his and other tenants' refrigerators. Finally, his pet Labrador/husky Sam, would bark and start pulling him toward the cellar whenever they were near it.

"If I had been a bit more fussy," he said, "and put more effort into finding out what was behind all that, maybe the dungeon would have been discovered much earlier."

On Friday, May 2, investigators began scanning the entire area around Josef Fritzl's house with sonar, looking for more underground dungeons. Bloodhounds were brought in to see if there were any bodies buried in the garden.

Police had by now discounted Fritzl's threats of laying deadly gas pipes into the cellar, and after installing new ventilation shafts to increase the oxygen, forensic technicians were busy filming, photographing and mapping every inch of it.

They had also determined that the area where Elisabeth and her three children were held captive only accounted for a third of the massive underground extensions Fritzl had excavated.

"The other two-thirds were constructed, but were bricked up," revealed Chief Inspector Polzer. "This area is now being examined with a sonar probe. We have ruled out other dungeons or prisoners. However, we want to carry out a full investigation, so we are opening up the entire basement."

Polzer also said that Fritzl had meticulously kept paperwork for everything. Investigators had uncovered design plans for his dungeon, as well as many years of receipts documenting purchases of food, furniture, appliances and clothing for his cellar family.

With the possibility of an insanity plea, prosecutors were now looking for evidence to prove otherwise.

"We can say that Fritzl is an unbelievably enterprising and effective man," said lead investigator Polzer, "who has many skills and is highly intelligent. His conduct during these twenty-four years does not indicate a person with diminished capacities. On the contrary—everything up to now would conflict with the idea of a person who is not all there."

CHAPTER 22

Under Siege

In the week since Josef Fritzl's arrest, his so-called "House of Horrors" had become one of the biggest international news stories in years. There was huge media interest, with each new daily development making front pages in newspapers as far away as China, India and Russia.

Consequently, the Fritzl family was now under siege at the Amstetten-Mauer clinic, as scores of photographers and news crews encamped outside. Reportedly there was a $1.5 million bounty for the first picture of Elisabeth, currently portrayed in an artist's rather gruesome impression of how she might have aged into a white-haired old woman.

After several incidents of photographers attempting to sneak through the clinic gates commando-style to snap photographs, the elite Austrian anti-terrorism Cobra Force had been drafted in, equipped with thermal-imaging night cameras and guard dogs. Over the next few days, seventeen photographers would be arrested trying to capture that elusive photograph that every news organization in the world was clamoring for.

One freelance photographer even donned an Austrian police officer's uniform, and brazenly attempted to walk into the clinic, before being apprehended. Another one put on camouflage gear and climbed a tree for a long-range shot of the Fritzl family before he was discovered.

On Saturday, clinic officials pleaded with journalists to back off, saying that publishing a photograph of Elisabeth could result in "secondary trauma," setting back her recovery for months.

"We're under siege from the press," said Mauer clinic spokesman Klaus Schwertner. "The original plan was to let them walk outside in the grounds, a tranquil and secluded place. But they cannot go outside. They're climbing trees to try and see in. They're literally storming the clinic."

Five miles across Amstetten, there were still more journalists and television crews stationed on a side street behind Ybbsstrasse 40, where they'd been for more than a week. Several neighbors across the street had rented out balconies to camera crews for exorbitant rates.

The entire area around the "Incest House" had become a ghoulish three-ring circus, as thousands of "catastrophe tourists" took a detour off the main A1 motorway to gawk at the house.

"I find this shocking," said Amstetten Deputy Mayor Ursula Puchebner. "I do not understand their motivation. It shows no respect for the victims."

But incredibly, with all the intense police activity around Ybbsstrasse, Rosemarie Fritzl's gray hatchback car remained parked just across from the family home, apparently still unnoticed by investigators. Visible in the back seat was a large color photograph of her granddaughter Lisa by an address book, just as she had left it more than a week ago.

When a local reporter asked police why it had not been examined, he was politely told to mind his own business.

It would be another few days before police towed it into headquarters for a forensic examination.

On Sunday, May 4, Amstetten Catholic church held a special Mass to pray for Elisabeth Fritzl and her children. It was a moving service, and afterwards the congregation signed a banner hung outside the church, showing support for the Fritzl family.

Forty-five miles away in St. Polten prison, Josef Fritzl was in solitary confinement, after his cellmate had threatened to murder him, reportedly having gone berserk after Fritzl calmly admitted imprisoning his own daughter as a sex slave.

"From experience," said prison governor Gunther Morwald, "we know that with sexual crimes where children are the victims, there is an increased need of protection for the prisoner."

The governor then described his notorious inmate as "unproblematic . . . calm, collected and alert."

That was in sharp contrast to Rudolf Mayer calling his client "a broken man," and telling reporters that Fritzl had been diagnosed as a schizophrenic by a prison psychiatrist who had interviewed him.

"My client is psychologically ill," said Mayer, who had visited him over the weekend, "and as a result is not responsible for his actions."

He confirmed that Fritzl remained under a twenty-four-hour suicide watch, describing him as "distraught" and "depressed."

"It is certainly hard for him in jail," said the attorney. "He is also very worried about all the threats.

Locking him up in jail is not the right thing to do. He needs proper psychological care."

It was also reported that Fritzl had begged his wife Rosemarie to visit him, so he could explain himself, but she had refused. Police had also announced their intention to re-interview her in the near future, to see if she had known anything about the cellar.

"We think Fritzl acted alone," said Chief Inspector Polzer, "but cannot exclude the possibility that someone else was aware of what was going on downstairs."

That day, Josef Fritzl was cleared of any involvement in the murder of Martina Posch, after furnishing an alibi. But now Lower Austrian police announced that he would be questioned about the August 1966 sex murder of 17-year-old Anna Neumayr, whose body was found in a cornfield in Pfaffstaett bei Mattinghofen, a few miles away from where he'd worked at the time.

Anna's brutal murder—with a captive bolt pistol—had occurred around the time that Fritzl had been suspected of attempted rape in Linz, and now detectives wanted to use DNA and other evidence to see if he was responsible.

Police said a photograph showing Fritzl in the area at the time of the killing had recently surfaced, and he was believed to have visited there every year, as he owned land there.

"We will investigate whether there is anything to indicate that Josef Fritzl was near the scene at the time," said a police spokesman.

That evening, Christoph Herbst, the Fritzl family's newly appointed attorney to handle their affairs, appeared on ORF Austrian television in a special program about the case.

"Elisabeth is to be admired," he said. "She's a very strong woman."

Herbst said real progress had been made, and it was "quite gratifying" to see how members of the family were now helping each other recover.

"It is good to see how Elisabeth and her children are getting on together," he said. "And the children are really getting on well together too. The effort of getting back to normal is visible."

But the Vienna-based psychologist Brigitte Lueger-Schuster, an expert in posttraumatic stress disorder, appeared on the same program, warning that recovery would be a long and painful process.

"There is a honeymoon phase after the event," she explained. "But the real test is to come. They will have to tackle piece by piece what they have had to go through, and come to terms with it."

Dr. Keith Ablow agreed that the healing process would not be easy.

"I think the road can be tremendously difficult," he said, "and it may not be possible to navigate it for each of these individuals. But think back to the Holocaust. There were kids raised in prison camps who went on to be free, to marry, to have careers and experience the joy in life. And so it's quite possible and always worth the effort."

Doctors were now slowing down the cellar family's medical treatment, after Elisabeth and Felix suffered a relapse. The staff had been opening the curtains of the family's wing a little more every day, to gradually get them used to sunlight, but it had proved too strong for their weak eyes to cope with.

"They have had a bit of a setback," explained Mauer clinic director Dr. Berthold Kepplinger. "We have now given them back their protective glasses."

That night in a radio interview broadcast, Rudolf Mayer confirmed that he was working on an insanity defense for his client. He said Josef Fritzl was suffering from a serious mental disorder and "didn't choose" to do what he did.

"I believe that the trigger was a mental disorder," said Mayer. "Because I can't imagine that someone has sex with his own daughter without having a mental disorder. Therefore he is not responsible for his actions."

The defender said psychiatric experts would now have to examine Fritzl, to decide if he was certifiably insane. That would mean that if he were to be convicted, he would serve out his time in the comparative comfort of a psychiatric institution instead of a tough prison.

"My client does not belong in a prison," said Mayer, "but rather in a closed psychiatric ward."

And he warned that if the St. Polten court–appointed forensic psychiatrist, scheduled to examine Fritzl the next morning, ruled him mentally competent, Mayer would immediately challenge the finding. For under Austrian law, the defense is entitled to a second psychiatric opinion.

"If I feel that the expert opinion does not correctly portray the personality of my client," said Mayer, "I will order another expert examination."

On Monday morning, as Kerstin Fritzl's condition showed a slight improvement, there were reports that police now feared she also might have been raped by

Josef Fritzl. London's *Daily Telegraph* claimed investigators believed that after he tired of her mother, Fritzl may have turned his daughter/granddaughter into his sex slave.

But Dr. Albert Reiter said it was impossible to examine her for signs of sexual abuse while she remained in a coma.

"Thank God she is slightly better," he said. "Her condition has stabilized and it is no longer life-threatening. We [are] slowly reducing the amount of drugs she is being given."

Asked whether Kerstin may have been another sexual victim, Chief Inspector Franz Polzer refused to answer directly, saying police now believed they had discovered what had driven Josef Fritzl to commit his terrible crimes.

"His motive was to re-create once again the situation he had with his first family, the legal family," explained Polzer. "But this time with a good-looking younger daughter."

But after more than twenty years imprisoned underground, the once-beautiful Elisabeth had prematurely aged, resembling her mother. So, had the 73-year-old sexual predator turned to the next generation of his family to satisfy his twisted lust?

At a press conference that afternoon, Chief Polzer revealed that Fritzl had spent at least six years obsessively planning and constructing his dungeon before taking Elisabeth prisoner. He had started by applying for planning permission to convert his cellar into a nuclear shelter soon after he had begun raping her.

"He planned her incarceration and prison in minute detail," Polzer explained. "He was obsessed and went to elaborate lengths . . . with the objective of keeping his daughter captive for a long time. This goes some way toward explaining how he was able to conceal his actions from the rest of the world for so long."

The next morning, the *Osterreich* newspaper revealed that Josef Fritzl had regularly patronized the Villa Ostende brothel in Linz since the 1970s, gaining a reputation as "an extreme pervert." A barman, identified only as Christioph R., said that many of the girls there would refuse him their services, as he was just too weird.

"He was bossy with everyone," said Christioph, who had worked there for more than six years. "People go there to relax and have fun."

District Governor Hans-Heinz Lenze confirmed the reports.

"All the prostitutes from Amstetten to St. Polten knew him," said Lenze. "And they told us he asked them to do terrible things."

CHAPTER 23

"I Could Have Killed Them All"

On Tuesday, May 6, Rudolf Mayer visited St. Polten jail to interview his client about what he had done and why. It would be Josef Fritzl's version of *Mein Kampf*, to be released to the media as a public relations exercise to show his "human side."

During the lengthy interview, Fritzl spoke of his strange relationship with his mother, admitting harboring sexual feelings toward her. He also talked of his pride in raising his downstairs family, his obsession with incest, and wanting to have a family with Elisabeth, who he called "my second wife."

Later many would question if his jailhouse interview was merely a cynical attempt to influence the Austrian judicial system, which was about to take the first legal step to decide whether he would go to prison or a hospital for the criminally insane.

"I come from a small family and grew up in a tiny flat in Amstetten," Fritzl began. "My father was somebody who was a waster, he never took responsibility and was just a loser that always cheated on my mother.

"My mother threw him out of the house when I was four, and she was quite right to do so. After that, it was only the two of us.

"My mother was a strong woman, she taught me

discipline and control and the values of hard work. She sent me to a good school so that I could learn a good trade, and she worked really hard, and took a very difficult job to keep our heads above water.

"When I say she was hard on me, she was only as hard as was necessary. She was the best woman in the world. I suppose you could describe me as her man, sort of. She was the boss at home and I was the only man in the house.

"It's complete rubbish to say my mother sexually abused me—my mother was respectable, extremely respectable. I loved her across all boundaries. I was totally in awe of her. Completely and totally in awe. That did not mean there was anything else between us, though. There never was and there never would have been."

When Mayer asked if he had ever fantasized about having sex with his mother, Fritzl took a long pause before answering.

"Yes, probably," he conceded. "But I was a very strong man, probably as strong as my mother. And as a result I was able to keep my desires under control.

"I became older, and that meant that when I went outside, I managed to meet other women. I had affairs with a few girls, and then a short while later I met Rosemarie."

Mayer then asked if Rosemarie shared anything in common with his mother.

"Absolutely nothing," he replied. "She had nothing in common with my mother . . . Well, perhaps there were a few similarities if I really think about it. I mean, Rosemarie was also a wonderful woman, is a wonderful woman. She is just a lot more shy, and weaker than my mother.

"I chose her because I had a strong desire then to

have lots of children. I wanted children that did not grow up like me as [a single child], I wanted children that always had someone else at their side to play with and to support.

"The dream of a big family was with me from when I was very, very small. And Rosemarie seemed to be the perfect mother to realize that dream. This is not a good reason to marry, but it is also true to say that I loved her and I still love her."

Mayer then asked about the circumstances of his 1967 rape conviction, for which he served an 18-month jail sentence.

"I do not know what drove me to do that," he replied. "It's really true I do not know why I did it, I always wanted to be a good husband and a good father."

His attorney then questioned him about neighbors' claims of him being a "brutal tyrant" at home.

"I always put a lot of value on good behavior and respect," he explained, "I admit that. The reason for this is that I belong to an old school of thinking that just does not exist today.

"I grew up in the Nazi times and that meant there needed to be control and the respect of authority. I suppose I took on some of these old values with me into later life—all subconsciously, of course.

"Yet despite that, I am not the monster that I am portrayed as in the media . . . I could have killed them all . . . then nothing would have happened. No one would ever have known about it."

Mayer asked how he would describe someone who kidnapped his own daughter, locking her up for twenty-four years in the cellar, repeatedly raping her and subjecting her to his brutal subjugation.

"On the face of it, probably as a beast or a monster," he admitted.

The only time Fritzl became angry was when his attorney mentioned Elisabeth's claims that he had begun molesting her as an 11-year-old child.

"That is not true," he snapped. "I am not a man that has sex with little children. I only had sex with her later, much later. It was when she was in the cellar by then, when she had been in the cellar for a long time."

He was then asked how much planning had gone into constructing the dungeon.

"Two, three years beforehand," he said. "That is true. I guess it must have been around 1981 or 1982 when I began to build a room in my cellar as the cell for her."

Then he proudly described how he had installed "a really heavy concrete-and-steel door," that operated electronically by keying in a numbered code by remote control. He had then plastered the walls to soundproof the dungeon, bringing in a small toilet, a bed and a cooking ring, as well as the fridge, electricity and lights.

He viewed the cellar as his "kingdom," which no one else could ever enter.

"I made it clear that this was my office, with various files and folders stored," he said. "And that was enough—everybody obeyed my rules."

His lawyer then asked why he had imprisoned Elisabeth in the first place.

"Ever since she entered puberty," he explained, "Elisabeth stopped doing what she was told. She just did not follow any of my rules anymore. She would go out all night in local bars, and come back stinking of alcohol and smoke.

"I tried to rescue her from the swamp, and I organized her a trainee job as a waitress, but sometimes there were days when she would not go to work.

"She even ran away twice and hung around with

persons of questionable moral standards, who were certainly not a good influence on her. I always had to bring her home, but she always ran away again. That is why I had to arrange a place where I gave her the chance—by force—to keep away from the bad influences of the outside world."

And Fritzl denied Elisabeth's claims to police that he had handcuffed her and kept her on a leash during the first few months of her twenty-four-year imprisonment.

"That was not necessary," he said. "My daughter had no chance to get away anyway. I guess after the kidnap, I got myself in a vicious circle, a vicious circle not just for Elisabeth, but also for me, from which there was no way out.

"With every week that I kept my daughter prisoner, my situation just got more crazy, and really, it is true, I often thought of if I should let her free or not. But I just was not capable of making a decision, even though, and probably because, I knew that every day made my crime that much worse.

"I was scared of being arrested, and that my family and everybody that knew me would know my crime. That was why I kept putting off the day I should make a decision, putting it off again and again. Eventually, after a time, it was just too late to bring Elisabeth back into the world.

"My desire to have sex with Elisabeth also got much stronger as time went by. We first had sex in spring 1985. I could not control myself anymore. At some stage somewhere in the night, I went into the cellar and laid her down on the bed and had sex with her. I knew that Elisabeth did not want it, what I did with her. The pressure to do the forbidden thing was just too big to withstand. It was an obsession with me."

Mayer then questioned him about what had happened after his daughter became pregnant.

"Elisabeth was, of course, very worried about the future," he said. "But I brought her medical books in the cellar, so that she would know when the day came what she had to do, and I arranged towels and disinfectants and nappies."

The attorney asked how he had felt after she gave birth to Kerstin and Stefan.

"I was delighted about the children," he replied. "It was great for me to have a second proper family in the cellar, with a good wife, and a few children."

Mayer then asked what would have happened to his captives if he had been killed during one of his lengthy vacations.

"I prepared well in this eventuality," he replied. "Every time I left the bunker, I switched on a timer that would definitely have opened the door to the cellar after a set time. If I had died, Elisabeth and the children would have been free."

Why, asked his lawyer, had he taken Lisa upstairs in May 1993, to bring her up there with Rosemarie?

"Elisabeth and I planned everything together," he claimed. "Because we both knew that Lisa, because of her poor health condition and the circumstances in the cellar, had no chance to live had she remained there."

He said he had brought the next two children—Monika and Alexander, born in 1994 and 1996—upstairs because they were "weak, difficult and often ill." Also, he said, there were "complications" caused by their births.

He then compared his two wives, saying Rosemarie was "the best mother in the world," while Elisabeth "was just as good a housewife and mother."

Fritzl then admitted that each new baby increased

his control over his daughter, as she no longer cared about her own life, doing everything he wanted for the children's sake.

He also spoke of bringing Elisabeth photographs and news about her children's life upstairs and their progress at school.

"After the birth of Felix at the end of 2002," he told Mayer, "I even gave Elisabeth a washing machine as a present, so that she did not have to wash her own clothes and that of the children by hand."

He said his upstairs children always called him "Daddy," although they knew he was their grandfather, whereas the ones downstairs referred to him as "Grandfather," as Elisabeth had never told them the truth.

Asked if his daughter had ever resisted his sexual advances, Fritzl said she had never screamed or tried to fight him off. And he seemed proud that she had taught their children to always be nice to Grandfather.

"I tried really hard, as much as possible, to look after my family in the cellar," he told Mayer. "When I went there I brought my daughter flowers, [the] children books and cuddly toys. I used to watch videos and adventure movies with the children, while Elisabeth used to cook for us. Then we used to sit at the table . . . with each other.

"We celebrated birthdays and Christmas in the cellar. I even brought a Christmas tree secretly into the cellar, and cakes and presents."

Mayer then asked if conditions in the cellar had adversely affected his captives' health.

"Yeah, sure," he admitted. "Elisabeth stayed strong, she caused me almost no problems, she never, ever complained, even when her teeth slowly went rotten and fell out of her mouth one after the other, and she suffered day and night with unbearable pain and could not sleep. She stayed strong for the children. But I saw the children were constantly getting weaker."

Why had he finally decided to release them at the beginning of 2008 as their health worsened? Mayer asked.

"I wanted to free Elisabeth, Kerstin, Stefan and Felix," he replied, "and to bring them back home. That was my next step. The reason is that I was getting older. I was finding it harder to move, and I knew that in the future I would no longer be able to care for my second family in the cellar. The plan was that Elisabeth and the children would explain that they were kept by a sect in a secret place."

The lawyer wondered if he believed this to be realistic that they wouldn't betray him.

"Sure, that was my hope, however unbelievable at that time," he said. "Despite that, there was always the risk that Elisabeth and the children would betray me. That did happen rather sooner than I expected, as the problem with Kerstin escalated."

Then, speaking of Kerstin's illness, which had led to the dungeon's demise, he said angrily, "She tore the clothes from her body and threw them in the toilet. Kerstin would not be alive today if it wasn't for me. I made sure that she got to the hospital."

He was then asked how he had prevented any escape attempts.

"It was not difficult," he replied. "I certainly did not need any physical violence. Elisabeth, Kerstin, Stefan and Felix accepted me as the head of the family completely, and they never trusted themselves to have the strength to attack me.

"And in any case, only I knew the number code of the remote control that would open the door to the cellar and to close it."

Fritzl denied threatening to gas them, but admitted, "I am sorry to say that I did tell them that they would never get past the door, because they would be electrocuted and they would die."

Mayer finally asked if he wanted to die now that he had been caught.

"No," he said, "I only want redemption. I always knew during those twenty-four years that what I was doing was wrong. I must have been mad to do something like that, but nevertheless I was not able to escape my double life. When I was upstairs, I was totally normal. I functioned well, I made money, took care of my family and only consciously thought about downstairs when I had to run errands for my second family.

"But at some point it became a matter of course for me that I led a double life in the basement of my house, and that I had to take care of a second wife and our children down there."

On Wednesday morning, State Prosecutor Christiane Burkheiser interrogated Josef Fritzl for two hours in his cell. The first interview was only about his personal circumstances, career and family background, and nothing else for the time being.

"He has proven to be remarkably cooperative," a St. Polten prosecutor's office spokesman told *Spiegel* Online. "We are waiting for the police to carry out further investigations before questioning him again."

A few hours later, the Fritzl case was raised in the Austrian Parliament during a motion debate on whether to introduce tougher penalties for rapists (including an idea from the far right to introduce physical or chemical castration), as well as not erasing criminal files for sex offenses after fifteen years.

The urgent call for the change in law came after the

disclosure that Fritzl had been allowed to officially adopt and foster three of Elisabeth's children despite being a convicted rapist.

Hours before the debate, Justice Minister Maria Berger finally admitted that Amstetten officials had been "gullible" in accepting Josef Fritzl's stories over the years. In an interview with Austria's *Der Standard* newspaper, she vowed it would never happen again.

"Looking at everything we know up to now," she said, "I can see a certain gullibility—especially when it comes to that tale that she had joined a sect, with which the suspect explained the disappearance of his daughter. Today, one would certainly pursue this more precisely."

The minister pledged to tighten Austrian adoption procedures to prevent another Josef Fritzl from manipulating the system.

"In general, adoptive parents are checked up thoroughly," she said. "One way to do this is to check the criminal record. Now we also want to make this compulsory when it comes to privileged adoptions by family members."

Reacting to this, Elisabeth's lawyer Christoph Herbst said he was examining the possibility of claiming compensation from debt-ridden Fritzl, who still had five properties in his name.

Late Wednesday night, five hundred people descended on Amstetten's town square for a further show of support for the Fritzl family. They unfurled a large banner made by schoolchildren, bearing the messages "Wishing You Strength on Your Path Through Life," "It Was Hell For You, Now We Wish You Lots of Sunshine" and, "We're With You."

But there were other signs displayed by citizens, pleading with the world's media to leave them alone.

"The town is ready to move on," said demonstration organizer Margarete Reisinger. "I'm here because this was one man, and it now reflects on all of us. I'm proud to be from Amstetten."

City official Hermann Gruber addressed the crowd, saying that the good people here today represented the *real* Amstetten, and not the evil of Josef Fritzl.

CHAPTER 24

"We, the Whole Family"

On Thursday, Josef Fritzl's bizarre *mea culpa* ran in the Austrian publication *News Magazin*, and was immediately picked up by the international press. But far from generating sympathy for him, it had the opposite effect, and was widely seen as cynical and delusional.

"I Could Have Killed Them All," was the headline in Germany's *Bild-Zeitung*, and "Dungeon Dad's Sick Defense," was the *New York Post*'s offering. The London *Sun* ran a front-page color picture of Fritzl sunbathing in a pair of red Speedos, with the headline, "I Lusted After My Mother."

The next morning, Josef Fritzl, wearing casual clothes, was brought, under heavy armed guard, though without handcuffs, to St. Polten court. There he joined his attorney, Rudolf Mayer, for a fifteen-minute hearing behind closed doors.

The judge remanded Fritzl for another month in custody while the investigation proceeded. During the hearing, Fritzl was told that he would most likely face a murder charge, putting him behind bars for the rest of his life.

"In Austria he could be charged with murder through negligence," explained Gerhard Sedlacek, a spokesman for the prosecutor's office. "It needs to be proved that the baby would have survived had he [gotten] proper medical attention. That carries a life sentence—and life means life."

Sedlacek told reporters that police were running down every single lead, forecasting that the investigation could take six months to complete.

"The investigation continues," said Sedlacek. "The charges against him will probably be filed this fall, when we expect the trial to begin."

Outside the court, defender Mayer said Fritzl wondered why none of his family had visited him and was missing his wife Rosemarie.

"Psychologically," Mayer told reporters, "my client is in a very bad way. But he does not complain. His biggest fear is how his children are faring without him. He wants to know how they're coping with it all."

A few hours later, Chief Inspector Franz Polzer held another press conference, announcing that investigators had discovered two new rooms in the cellar, sealed off with concrete. They had entered the rubble-filled rooms, thought to have been used as storage space during the cellar's construction.

"This prison was so complex, so extensive," said Polzer, "that it exhausted Mr. Fritzl's capabilities."

He said the investigation into the cellar and nearby grounds was almost complete, and they were now concentrating the search for human remains in the grounds outside.

"We have been using sniffer-dogs and ground radar," he said, "in order not to have to dig up the whole area."

Sunday was Austrian Mother's Day, and Elisabeth, her mother and her children celebrated together at the

Amstetten-Mauer clinic. They all sat down for a special lunch, and during the meal the children gave Elisabeth and Rosemarie flowers from the clinic gardens as presents.

It had now been two weeks since the family had reunited, and everybody appeared to be bonding well. The closed-off clinic wing had been divided into areas, with the children sharing bedrooms. Lisa and Monika slept together in one space, while the older brothers Stefan and Alexander slept together in another. Elisabeth shared her bed with Felix, who needed constant reassurance.

Since gaining her freedom, Elisabeth had surprised everyone by her sheer strength and determination to heal her family.

"Elisabeth is really an impressive person," said family lawyer Christoph Herbst at a press conference that day. "She is very strong . . . a tower of strength [and] happy now for the first time. Her biggest wish now is to have the family together and to have the best for her children. They need time to heal and grow together. Everything else is secondary to her. She tells her family that all she longs for is a normal life. That's her only wish."

The attorney dispelled media reports about the toll all the years of imprisonment had taken on Elisabeth's physical appearance.

"Some people who hear the story think Elisabeth is like something from a horror film," he said. "But rumors that she had no teeth and cannot talk are not true. If you met her, you wouldn't realize what she has been through . . . Elisabeth is an attractive woman, and does not look old or drawn in some way, like it is speculated in the media."

He ridiculed other rumors circulating in the press about the family.

"If a family member were sitting here next to us," he said, "you would not find a difference. One does not notice any of the things that were implied or believed by people outside."

Herbst also revealed that, during their time in the cellar, Elisabeth had scrupulously recorded the dates of birth for all her children on scraps of paper. And next week, Kerstin, Stefan and Felix would all be receiving birth certificates and Austrian passports, so they would now legally exist.

Updating reporters on the family's progress, Herbst said that little Felix was making exceptional progress, recently seeing rain for the first time through the clinic window.

"Unfortunately he was unable to go out," said Herbst. "He didn't know what rain was, and was fascinated by it. He is a lively and lovely little fellow, and delights in every new discovery."

As the youngest of the cellar children, Felix would probably have the best chance of leading a normal life one day, but his older brother Stefan was having a much tougher time. While the little boy was now learning to run, as well as riding a new bicycle—things he could never do in the dungeon—Stefan had trouble even standing up, lacking basic motor skills and coordination. He spent his days staring at the fish in his aquarium, just as he had done in the cellar.

Their upstairs siblings were also having their own set of difficulties. Lisa, Monika and Alexander all missed their friends at school, angry that their normal life had been turned upside down.

"They cannot go out," explained Herbst, as their

psychiatrists had advised against them going back to school for the foreseeable future, "so for them, life is completely different. They don't have the freedom they had before. They cannot see their friends, they cannot meet their classmates. This is very hard for them. And they are asking, when they can meet them again? When can they go to school again? And we all hope that this will happen pretty soon."

In the meantime, the three upstairs children were being privately tutored, ensuring that they didn't fall behind in their schoolwork. They also spent time watching Disney DVDs and reading the hundreds of letters of support pouring into the clinic from all over the world.

Elisabeth was so moved by all this good will towards the family, she decided a response was required. So, after discussing it with doctors, she called everyone together to initiate a moving family project.

For the next two days in collective therapy, Elisabeth, Rosemarie and the children all worked hard, preparing a huge colorful thank-you poster, full of rainbows, hearts and smiling faces, to be displayed in a store window in Amstetten town square for the world to see.

Elisabeth wrote across the top of the poster:

We, the whole family, would like to use this opportunity to thank you all for sympathizing with our fate. Your empathy is helping us to go through these difficult times, and it shows us that there also are good and honest people. We hope that there will be a time when we can return to normal life.

Then, one by one, they each traced different colored crayons around their hands and fingers, writing individual messages inside their outlined palms. A large heart at the bottom was drawn for Kerstin, who remained unconscious in Amstetten hospital.

Elisabeth's message, written inside her green hand outlines, said:

I wish for—the recovery of my daughter Kerstin, the love of my children, the protection of my family, for people with a big heart and compassion.

Then Lisa, 16, took a red crayon and wrote:

Wishes: health, that everything goes well, love, happiness.
Misses: Kerstin, school, friends, fresh air, Class 1C.

Stefan's message was in purple:

I miss my sister. I am enjoying freedom and my family. I like the sun, the fresh air and the nature.

Then in green crayon, 12-year-old Alexander wrote:

I desire freedom, strength and power and the sun. I miss the fire brigade and sister Kerstin.

His 14-year-old sister Monika took a purple crayon, writing inside her palm prints, besides a smiley face:

Wishes: that Kerstin gets better, lots of love, that everything is soon past.
Misses: fire brigade, music school, friends, school, Kerstin.

Little Felix did his in green:

> *I dream of playing with the other children, running in the meadows, riding in cars, playing ball, swimming, sleigh rides, and playing with other children.*

Finally, Rosemarie Fritzl wrote her message in red and purple crayon, signing it "Oma":

> *I wish to be able to live in peace with my children, with much strength and with God's help I miss my dear friends and my freedom.*

Rosemarie was still coming to terms with what had happened. As detectives prepared to interview her again, it was revealed that on discovering the truth, she had suffered a nervous breakdown. She was now being treated for severe heart problems, believed to have been caused by all her years of stressful living with her husband.

"With new details emerging daily of what was going on under her own house," said a police source, "she's been unable to take it in."

Chief Inspector Franz Polzer confirmed that Rosemarie would soon be questioned again, emphasizing that she was not under suspicion.

"What woman would stay silent," he asked, "if she knew that her husband had seven children with his daughter, and was holding her in the cellar?"

On Monday, May 12, doctors decided to slowly reduce Kerstin's medication, to ease her out of the coma. After her condition had stabilized a few days earlier, she had started getting stronger and stronger. Now her doctors were hopeful that she might make a full recovery. But their big fear was whether she had suffered any brain damage, as severe cramping brought on by her infection might have starved her brain of oxygen.

"The medication keeping her in an artificial coma is being slowly reduced," explained Dr. Albert Reiter. "This is the first phase in the process of eventually waking her up. How long this will take is something we cannot say."

Doctors viewed her mother as being crucial to her recovery. So every day, Elisabeth would be disguised as a nurse in a red wig with a ponytail, walking out through the front gates and past news photographers, who never recognized her. Then an ambulance would drive her to the hospital, where she would spend hours gently talking to her daughter, who was still catheterized and hooked up to various breathing and nutrition tubes.

"During this period," said Dr. Reiter, "it was extremely important that Kerstin's mother was coming to the bed on a regular basis to motivate her."

CHAPTER 25

Frankenstein

On Monday, May 12, as police allowed tenants to briefly return to Ybbsstrasse 40 to move out their stuff, a team of court-appointed psychiatrists started examining Josef Fritzl, to see if he was truly insane. It would be the beginning of weeks of testing to establish if he was aware of the horror he had inflicted on his family. Then they would have to decide where he would spend the rest of his life.

Dr. Adelheid Kastner, the 46-year-old head of the forensic department of the Linz psychiatric clinic, had been selected to lead a team of experts to interview Fritzl in depth about all areas of his life and behavior. Her team would also conduct special tests to determine if he was suffering from any psychiatric disorder and try to explain his abhorrent behavior.

Before the first round of testing began, Dr. Kastner, who has studied an estimated five hundred murderers, told reporters that she would not be "pressured" into making a diagnosis.

"What is special about this case is the worldwide media interest," she said. "And the case itself is without precedent. But I will treat it like any other, and if my results do not conform to public expectation, that is not my concern. I always go into an assessment interview neutral and professional. It is not up to me to condemn."

Dr. Kastner asserted that she would study every part of Fritzl's personality, saying it would be difficult for him to feign insanity.

"In a very few cases," she explained, "some of the subjects have tried to fake a mental condition in a bid to appear unfit for trial. But that is a rare occurrence and it can hardly be successful, as any condition that would deem a person unfit for trial is very complex and with a number of symptoms."

The length of time needed to complete her tests would depend on how cooperative her subject would be.

"The analysis could take anything between a single session to several days or even weeks," she explained. "I've had a few cases where subjects have refused to cooperate."

There was much speculation in the press as to what had driven Josef Fritzl to commit his terrible crimes. One popular theory was that he was suffering from so-called "Frankenstein syndrome."

"He was like Dr. Frankenstein," German psychiatrist Dr. Christian Lüdke told the London *Mail*. "Fritzl was delusional and enjoyed being the master of life and death, exercising the ultimate power.

"He enjoyed this fantasy of playing God. He was like Dr. Frankenstein, fathering the children, then deciding their fate and controlling all they did. This man is the personification of the terrifying power of evil—the devil."

Although it is impossible to obtain a true psychological profile without many hours of face-to-face interviews, forensic psychiatrist Dr. Keith Ablow believes that Fritzl's growing up in Nazi Germany and the relationship with his mother are key to understanding him.

"So what kind of questions would I ask him?" said Dr. Ablow, noting that as he has never interviewed Fritzl, all his reflections represent theories. "What were your experiences in Germany at that time? What did you see happen to children? Did you have any fantasies about what you'd like to do if you had all that power?

"Equally, how did your mother provoke these feelings in you, that you'd like to have a relationship with her? Did she know about these feelings? Did she punish you for the feelings? Were there times when she knew you to be having sexual feelings that weren't about her?"

The next morning, a team of ten forensic investigators began examining the handiwork Fritzl had put into the cellar construction, to determine if he had done it alone or had any outside assistance. It had already been calculated that in building the dungeon, Fritzl had somehow moved 197 tons of earth—the equivalent of seventeen truckloads—and then somehow disposed of it without raising suspicions.

Equally baffling was how Fritzl had brought a washing machine, fridge and two beds into the cellar over the years, without anyone noticing.

They were also paying special attention to the electric installations, plumbing and gas lines, as well as the eight electronic security doors. And they now planned to break through old walls, to reach some hidden ones revealed by the sonar probes.

Eventually police would discover many rooms of all sizes in the cellar. One of particular interest contained a cache of diaries, invoices and other paperwork that the obsessive Fritzl had kept locked away for years. These would provide an in-depth look at how the dungeon was constructed, as well as other shocking revelations about Fritzl's twisted sexual history.

"He kept information going back more than twenty-four years," said a police spokesman. "He was extremely careful. Everything will now need to be checked."

Another team of highly trained specialists, wearing state-of-the-art Kappler protective suits, had also begun clearing out the dungeon. Over the next few days they would remove piles of trash, including dozens of empty cans of Fritzl's favorite Skol Lager, empty pizza and cereal boxes, and takeaway containers. Everything would then be transported to a police laboratory to be examined forensically.

The investigators worked under the constant gaze of tourists, now coming from as far as Germany and Hungary to make the pilgrimage to the Fritzl house and be photographed in front of it.

There were also reports that a local entrepreneur was operating bus tours from Tyrol into Amstetten, 250 miles away, stopping briefly in front of the house, before going back again.

"It's bad enough [with] journalists and TV crews," said one angry Amstetten resident, "but now there is this ghoulish tourism. It is appalling, we just want to be left in peace."

On Wednesday morning, Amstetten residents awoke to discover the Fritzl family thank-you poster on display in a storefront window in the main square. As word of it spread, the entire town descended on the square to see it for themselves, with many being moved to tears.

"The initiative . . . came from the family themselves," explained attorney Herbst. "It is their wish to thank the community for the support."

Later that day, Amstetten-Mauer clinic director Dr. Berthold Kepplinger held a press conference, saying the family would have to remain at the clinic for several more months at the least. When they were well enough to go out into the world, they would be given new identities, similar to being in a witness protection program.

"In order to give them a good start in their new life," said Dr. Kepplinger, "they all need to be very carefully protected and very slowly introduced to the real world, and to each other."

He said integrating the two sets of Fritzl children together had "gone extremely well," and they had now settled into a routine of playing together and painting. The family had also been given a computer, which was mainly being used for games.

Each day, the family met as a group to discuss how to move on with their lives.

"Apart from the psychiatric support of both the adults and the children," said Dr. Kepplinger, "we have started the first sessions of family therapy. These are primarily dealing with the issues of planning their future life."

On the more immediate front, Dr. Kepplinger said, Elisabeth, Stefan and Felix would also need additional therapy, to help them fully adjust to daylight, after spending their lives in the badly lit cellar. They would also undergo intensive physiotherapy and ergotherapy, to help them adapt to the larger spaces they now moved around in.

They were also receiving therapy to help them climb stairs and manage other physical activities they never had to do before. They would receive immunization shots, usually given to newborn babies, to build up their resistance to germs and bacteria in the outside world.

One treatment for the downstairs children was learning how to play. Therapists were shocked to find that

Stefan and Felix had absolutely no concept of "play," after spending their entire lives in the claustrophobic cellar. Elisabeth was now showing them how to swim and run—though Stefan had problems even standing up.

Experts designed customized treatments for individual family members, who each had a unique set of issues and problems to overcome.

"We are making every effort to give them what they need as a group or as individuals," said Dr. Kepplinger, "and we are carefully monitoring progress."

But these different treatments were already causing problems. The three "normal" upstairs children, now being isolated twenty-four hours a day in a hospital ward, were becoming increasingly frustrated and resentful, while their mother and downstairs siblings needed a far "slower pace of life," requiring peace and quiet.

"[They] are extremely different," said Dr. Kepplinger. "They have lived different lives, at different speeds, and both are having to adjust to the here and now. While for one set, even the smallest details are interesting, for the others, they're dull. For one lot, seeing a large cloud float by is a major event, for their upstairs siblings it is just boring."

Refusing to elaborate further, Dr. Kepplinger observed that Josef Fritzl's female children had a far different view of their father than their male siblings.

Once again he appealed to the media to stop harassing the family, after a clinic security officer had been badly injured by a photographer trying to break into the hospital. Ultimately, more than twenty photographers, mostly English, would be caught attempting to sneak into the clinic.

"This madness has to end," said the doctor. "The family needs time and peace. The protection of their privacy is of enormous importance for the success of the therapy. We are doing everything we can to protect the family from external stress."

Family lawyer Christoph Herbst said the "aggressive" media were effectively imprisoning Elisabeth, Stefan and Felix for a second time.

"The children would like to go out in the open," he said. "They have never experienced rain in their lives, nor have they felt fresh air. They're incredibly curious about everything around them, and they would like to touch the trees and the plants in the hospital gardens. But they are unable to leave the floor they are residing [on]."

Herbst said the family was now considering moving abroad under new identities.

"They are being hunted by the media," he said. "The family cannot live a normal life in Austria. I'm looking at the options and weighing up opportunities."

A few days later, Austrian authorities completed the official documents, providing new identities for Rosemarie, Elisabeth and her six children. All that was now needed were signatures to activate the new ID papers from the Amstetten district council.

That week's edition of the German magazine *Bunte* carried a major interview with Natascha Kampusch, who revealed that she had now bought Wolfgang Priklopil's house, which had been her prison for eight years. She said it would be therapeutic for her to own the house, to protect it from vandals or being demolished.

She had now been back to the scene of her horrific ordeal for the first time since her dramatic August 2006 escape.

"It is not as threatening as it was back then," she said. "But it is still a house of horrors for me."

The beautiful 20-year-old, soon to launch her own

Austrian cable television talk show, gave her own unique perspective on the Fritzl case, which mirrored her own.

"My stomach churned when I saw the pictures," she said. "I felt really sick. All the emotions that I've carefully tried to suppress were suddenly there again. It's very stressful."

After closely following the case, she described Josef Fritzl as "self-loving" and a "serious egoist," saying she was angry about his statement to the media.

"He's a liar," she said. "He doesn't care about anyone but himself, and it's monstrous for him to claim that he loves his wife and his daughter . . . what he did was sick."

She offered to personally help Elisabeth and her family with their healing, using her own similar experiences, but only if they needed her.

"If they don't want my help," she said, "then I'm not going to force myself on them. In my case, you wonder how a total stranger can possibly take a child away from [his or her] parents, and to put a whole family through such severe trauma. But this Fritzl did that to his own child, to his own family. That is even more unbelievable."

She warned that healing would take a long time, saying that even after nearly two years out of her cellar, she was still being helped by doctors, psychologists, social workers.

"It's a very dark past," she explained. "It's as if I lost my memory and have now started a completely new life."

On Thursday, May 15, Kerstin Fritzl woke up from her coma. Dr. Albert Reiter had been making his morning rounds when he saw his patient suddenly open her eyes and smile at him.

"It was an amazing moment," he recalled. "She opened her eyes and showed emotional reactions. We smiled at her and she smiled back at us."

The doctors had wanted Elisabeth to be there when she regained consciousness, as Kerstin had never seen anyone apart from her mother, two brothers and her father Josef Fritzl. But Elisabeth was told the good news immediately, and drove straight to the hospital to be at her daughter's bedside. Everybody breathed a huge sigh of relief, as it appeared Kerstin had not suffered any brain damage.

For the next two weeks, Elisabeth and the doctors were constantly at Kerstin's bedside, talking to her and giving her medication as she grew stronger by the day.

"It was very important that Elisabeth was there to motivate her," said Dr. Reiter, "and get her to participate in some of the things we asked her to participate in. That was so difficult with all the different tubes going into her neck and body, and catheters and all those things."

The doctors' main concerns, during those crucial first days, were to have Kerstin breathing on her own and be able to swallow solid food again.

"We mobilized her," explained the doctor. "We put her up in bed, and helped her prepare to be able to swallow foods, so she didn't choke, especially with the tubes still in her neck. So we were preparing her for the removal of the breathing tube."

It would be another two weeks until she could finally be taken off the respirator and start the next stage of her recovery.

Later that day, Chief Inspector Franz Polzer revealed that Josef Fritzl had been cruelly bluffing Elisabeth and his children for years, and there was no mechanism to release lethal gas into the cellar. He had also not installed any mechanism to open the cellar doors in the event of his death.

Chief Polzer said the investigation was almost complete, and police would soon be inspecting the 600-pound steel-and-reinforced-concrete door.

"It is clear," said Polzer, "that the suspect displayed a high degree of professionalism when he assembled it."

Police also released a postcard from Rosemarie Fritzl, dated April 21 during her Italian vacation, proving that her husband had delayed taking Kerstin to the hospital until she had left—which could have meant the difference between her life and death.

It also strengthened the police view that Rosemarie had absolutely no knowledge of what was going on under her nose.

A forensic search of Fritzl's paperwork had also shown that his real intention in bringing Lisa, Monika and Alexander upstairs was monetary gain. He was making at least $60,000 a year in perfectly legal Austrian state subsidies.

"They were cash cows for him," an investigator close to the case told the London *Sun*. "Everything he did was not out of concern for them, but to get money."

By Saturday, it was clear that the European paparazzi were ignoring Dr. Kepplinger's pleas to leave the family alone. Late Thursday night, one British photographer, seeking the reported $1 million bounty, almost succeeded in scaling the third balcony next to the sealed area where the family lived. But he was spotted by a nurse, whose screams alerted security staff, who caught him after a struggle, during which one guard fell from the balcony and was severely injured.

Shortly afterwards, a male nurse was caught attempting to sell a cell phone photograph to a magazine for $442,000. This led to the clinic banning all fifteen hospital employees with access to the family from carrying any phones or cameras. A letter was sent to all clinic staff, warning of immediate legal action if anyone was caught abusing their position.

It was also revealed that Elisabeth, Stefan and Felix had disguised themselves, managing to slip past photographers and spend a few hours playing in a nearby park. After seeing trees for the first time in his life, Felix had announced that when he grew up, he wanted to become a gardener.

"He was simply so fascinated by them," said one of the family's security guards, Franz Prankl, "and could not believe how huge they grew."

During the trip, which was closely monitored by doctors, the two boys, wearing dark sunglasses, marveled at the trees and grass and a fish pond.

On the way back to the clinic, they all stopped off at McDonald's—which Felix had only seen on television advertisements in the cellar, always being told it did not really exist and was only fiction. The little boy was ecstatic, eating his first Happy Meal.

The family had also received a personal invitation from Austrian-born movie superstar Arnold Schwarzenegger, to visit him in Hollywood, as soon as they were well enough. The California governor had reportedly read about the tragedy and wanted to do something to help.

"He will pay for it privately, and Elisabeth and the children will be personal guests," a Schwarzenegger source told London's *Daily Star*. "These children have been prisoners all their lives. Can you imagine how they'd react to Disneyland or a trip to Universal Studios?"

And movie star Ben Affleck had also weighed in

about the Fritzl case. During an interview to promote his directorial debut in a movie about child abduction called *Gone Baby Gone*, he was asked what should happen to people who criminally abuse children.

"Emotionally, I think the Austrian sex offender Josef Fritzl should be killed," he declared.

Exactly a month after Josef Fritzl had brought Kerstin out of the cellar, Austrian police announced that they were investigating him for a third unsolved sex-related murder. Nine months earlier, 42-year-old Czech prostitute Gabriele Supekova had been found dead near the Austrian border, a few miles away from where Fritzl had been vacationing at the time.

CHAPTER 26

Miracle

On Monday, May 19, Austrian newspapers announced that Elisabeth Fritzl would give a television interview about her twenty-four-year cellar ordeal. It was reported that she would tell her story to Christoph Feurstein, the same Austrian journalist who had conducted the landmark 2006 interview with Natascha Kampusch.

It was also reported that after "marathon negotiations" between ORF TV and Fritzl family lawyer Christoph Herbst, Elisabeth's interview would be broadcast the following Monday night. According to the report, the family stood to make millions of dollars from global syndication.

But less than twenty-four hours later, attorney Herbst totally dismissed the reports as erroneous, saying that Elisabeth hadn't even spoken to the police yet.

"At this stage, there are no plans whatsoever," he said. "A TV appearance by Elisabeth Fritzl is not planned at all. I am receiving many offers from various international media, but it is not in the family's best interest to go public."

Two days later, as investigators began staging "scream tests" from Josef Fritzl's soundproofed dungeon, to ascertain if anyone could have heard anything upstairs, reports from St. Polten jail suggested that he was now showing some remorse, after his first exploratory interviews with Dr. Adelheid Kastner.

"Fritzl's mood has changed dramatically in the past three weeks," London's *Daily Mirror* quoted a source inside the jail as saying. "When he first arrived, he was arrogant and unrepentant. But now he's a broken man. He cries all night and has lost a lot of weight—he's wasting away."

Since his arrest, Fritzl's only visitor had been an unidentified family friend. But now, through his attorney Rudolf Mayer, he had again requested Rosemarie and Elisabeth visit him.

"He told his legal team," said the source, " 'I want to see my family to explain things and find out how they are. I'm worried about them.' "

Elisabeth's lawyer Christoph Herbst said that she was now considering trying to recoup some of the estimated $1.5 million in therapy his family will need to recover.

"We have discussed if we want to sue him for damages," confirmed Herbst. "This is a decision that has to be taken by Elisabeth. It is quite difficult to understand Herr Fritzl's financial affairs, as he alone was in charge of his business. He owns several properties in and around Amstetten, but there are mortgages on some of them amounting to several millions. We are now trying to determine whether the sale of these properties would leave some profit after covering the debts."

Herbst speculated as to whether Fritzl had a secret fortune cunningly stashed away, saying it might be many months until he could be questioned about his financial affairs.

"If he was able to keep such a dark secret from the

world," said Herbst, "he could also have been able to keep his financial dealings confidential."

Soon after regaining consciousness, doctors gave Kerstin a CD player and headphones to help motivate her, as well as some CDs by Robbie Williams, whom she had first seen on television in the dungeon.

A few nights later, Dr. Albert Reiter discovered the teenager "almost dancing" in bed to the English rock star's music, although she was still attached to breathing tubes.

"She listened to Robbie Williams until three a.m.," Dr. Reiter recalled, "until I had to put a bit of a dampener on it. But that was the point in time where I said we should go ahead with steps to get her mobile."

Three days later, at 9:00 a.m. on Sunday, June 1, Amstetten hospital doctors removed the breathing tube from Kerstin's mouth, as her mother Elisabeth looked on nervously. As Kerstin took her very first breath of fresh air outside the dungeon, she gave an angelic smile.

"I said to Kerstin, 'Hello, Kerstin,'" recalled Dr. Albert Reiter. "And Kerstin told me 'Hello' back."

This was a giant first step in Kerstin's miraculous recovery from the edge of death, and from then on, things moved fast.

During the next critical phase of her recovery, Elisabeth assumed the role of life coach to her daughter. Every day she encouraged and motivated her to follow the doctor's instructions, to start using her muscles again and get stronger.

After more than six weeks in a coma, Kerstin was suffering from serious bed rest syndrome, and it was vital she exercise, to prevent bone and muscle atrophy.

"After the removal of the breathing tube," said Dr.

Reiter, "things were progressing rapidly. [Her mother's presence] had an immensely positive effect."

Kerstin now had to be taught how to swallow food and speak again, having been connected to the respirator for so long. And several days later, she enjoyed her first meal, tasting fresh fruit for the first time in her life.

Dr. Reiter said that, although there was some damage to her internal organs, Kerstin was now expected to make a complete recovery.

"This is quite astonishing and a great relief after everything that she has been through," he said.

But although she was making good physical progress, her fragile mental condition would be another thing entirely.

That night, Natascha Kampusch debuted her own Austrian cable television show, featuring former Formula 1 world-racing champion Nikki Lauda as her first guest. To promote her new show, she gave what was billed as her first-ever major newspaper interview with the London *Times*, again drawing parallels between herself and the Fritzls. In both horrific cases, she believed, the perpetrators were "blind with mother love."

"[Josef Fritzl] idolized his mother to an abnormal degree," she explained, "and that's what my abductor was like. He was very attached to his mother. Regardless of what I did, he would always say, 'My mother does it better.'"

On Friday, June 6, Josef Fritzl appeared in St. Polten court, where a judge remanded him in custody for a further two months. At a closed-door hearing, the state prosecutor's office said that more time would be needed to complete the investigation. It was also disclosed that DNA evidence conclusively proved Josef Fritzl had acted alone without an accomplice.

Meanwhile, sources inside St. Polten prison revealed that "Das Inzest Monster" had received more than two hundred love letters from women. Many of them offered romance, telling him he was "good at heart" and just plain misunderstood. But the love letters were being far outweighed by the sacks of hate letters also arriving each day.

Fritzl now stayed in his cell twenty-three-and-a-half hours a day, for fear of being attacked by inmates. He exercised his right to go outside for thirty minutes each day to sunbathe.

A week later, the narcissistic Fritzl requested a supply of anti-aging cream from prison officials, and also complained of chest pains and stomachaches.

"Herr Fritzl usually sits there watching television all day, especially news programs about him," said prison spokesman Lieutenant Colonel Erich Huber-Guensthofer. "To be honest, other than the trips to the doctor, and the request for face creams, he gives us no trouble."

On Saturday, the much-anticipated European Soccer Championships started, as co-host Austria hoped it would divert the eyes of the world from the embarrassing Fritzl case.

"Josef Fritzl . . . caused a scandal that shamed the nation," wrote the Associated Press. "Euro 2008—an event that's second only to the World Cup across this football-obsessed continent—will provide a welcome opportunity for some desperately needed merrymaking."

Like everyone else in Austria, the Fritzl family were all fanatical supporters of the home team. And down in the dungeon, Josef Fritzl had always enjoyed watching a game with Stefan, Felix and Kerstin, while Elisabeth was washing the dishes and cleaning.

Now a plasma television had been brought into their Mauer clinic ward, so they could watch every game. This was the first time doctors had allowed them to watch any television.

"We felt it wise not to let them view the TV coverage," explained Dr. Kepplinger, "as seeing reports about themselves could cause considerable distress. The ban is being lifted each time there is a game, so that the family can watch together, as one of the exercises designed to help them become a stronger family."

And ironically, just forty-five miles away in St. Polten prison, their former jailer, Josef Fritzl, was watching the same soccer games in his cell.

The next morning, Kerstin took her first steps in the ICU department, helped by her mother and Dr. Reiter. A few hours later, she was discharged from intensive care and taken by ambulance to the Mauer clinic to be reunited with the rest of her family.

When they arrived, Elisabeth took her eldest daughter's arm, helping her walk into the ward, where her brothers and sisters were waiting expectantly.

"For us it was a very special moment," recalled Dr. Reiter, who'd first admitted Kerstin into intensive care, and had become part of the family. "The mother was able to walk with Kerstin, the two of them literally stepping forward into a new life."

Now Kerstin met her grandmother Rosemarie and siblings Monika, Lisa and Alexander for the first time since their father had snatched them away as babies. She was also thrilled to be reunited with Stefan and Felix.

"It was a miracle," said family lawyer Christoph Herbst, who witnessed it. "It was a truly touching and happy moment. It was everyone's—and especially Kerstin's—great wish to be reunited. The family can at last come together."

To aid her recovery, doctors gave her a CD player and headphones, and some CDs by her favorite singer, Robbie Williams. Kerstin had become a huge fan of his music, saying she wanted to go to one of his concerts as soon as she was well enough.

A few days earlier, Austrian newspapers had reported that aging Josef Fritzl was suffering from a heart condition and might not live long enough to go to trial. Prosecutors had warned it could be months before Elisabeth, Stefan and Felix would be able to be interviewed by police, delaying the trial for up to two years.

When Elisabeth learned this, she was horrified, saying that she wanted to talk to prosecutors as soon as possible, vowing to do everything in her power to stop her father from evading justice.

CHAPTER 27

A New Start

On Wednesday, June 11, dozens of television crews from all over the world crowded into a small hotel dining room in Zeillern, a seven-minute drive from Amstetten. They had been summoned to a press conference, where Dr. Albert Reiter would announce Kerstin Fritzl's miraculous recovery.

"These first moments were the end of a very long ordeal and the start of a long road," said an obviously emotional Dr. Reiter, in a cracking voice.

Describing Kerstin's dramatic recovery as "a miracle," he recounted how she had first opened her eyes on May 15, and went on to describe her stunning progress, leading to the reunion with her family two weeks later.

"It was an extraordinary moment for me last Sunday," said the doctor, "when Kerstin, holding my arm, and I were able to walk through the door into a new home, crossing the threshold into a new life. Certainly for all of us, our Kerstin's good recovery has been a major relief."

Asked what had caused Kerstin's sickness, Dr. Reiter said he was still uncertain, but it could have been an epileptic seizure.

"We've so far been unable to ascertain the definite cause of organ failure," he said. "But it's probable that a small [untreated] inflammation triggered the failure of one of her major organs."

He said Kerstin's lungs appeared to have failed after she'd suffered an epileptic fit and bitten her tongue, leading to blood getting into her lungs.

Then, responding to a reporter's question about any requests Kerstin had made, Dr. Reiter said that after the breathing tube had been removed, she'd asked to go to a Robbie Williams concert.

"Now of course, it's very important that her condition will stabilize further. And further therapeutic steps are already being planned, certainly in the area of immune system strength."

Finally, he thanked hospital staff who had thwarted the paparazzi by smuggling Elisabeth past them to her daughter's bedside each day. He also thanked the catering department for brewing him all the cups of strong coffee he'd needed to function.

But on a more serious note, Dr. Reiter refused to discuss fears that Kerstin may have been sexually abused by her father, observing that medical examinations conducted while she was in intensive care had been inconclusive on the matter.

In June, the Fritzl family moved into a spacious villa, well hidden within the grounds of the Amstetten-Mauer clinic, embarking on the next step in the long healing process. Over the last few days, removal vans had quietly arrived at their new home, unloading seven beds, a lounge suite, a refrigerator, microwave, washing machine and toys.

Doctors hoped that by taking them away from a hospital atmosphere, they would be able to lead a more normal life. It would be that family's first home together, after spending more than two months at the clinic.

The secret move was also made to evade the press. The private security force patrolling the grounds of the clinic around the clock was disbanded also, saving the Amstetten council thousands of dollars a day.

Family life soon settled into an easy routine. Each morning Rosemarie and Elisabeth got up early to prepare breakfast, helped by the clinic staff.

After breakfast, Kirsten received physiotherapy while Felix played Chinese checkers and other board games with his doting grandmother. In another room, the four older children had classes with their respective tutors. Stefan, who had been taught basic mathematics and German grammar by his mother, surprised his teacher with how advanced he was under the circumstances.

After lunch, the family rested or had free time to do what they wanted. Stefan had exchanged the aquarium for computer games, tutored by his younger brother Alexander. And the two cellar brothers loved walking through the local botanical gardens, looking at nature, still wearing sunglasses to protect their eyes from harmful UV rays.

Most days Elisabeth's sister Gabrielle and other relatives came to visit, often bringing their children along.

"She has children of a similar age," said Christoph Herbst, "and the clinic becomes a madhouse while the children play together."

But in early June, the whole family gathered at night in front of their widescreen television, to watch Euro 2008 soccer—or football, as it's called in Europe. The excited children cheered so loudly for their favorite teams that Elisabeth had to keep them in order.

On Monday, June 16, they all watched Austria's crucial game against Germany in Vienna. The children were upset when the Austrian team was knocked out of the championships, losing 1–0 to Germany, who went on to win Euro 2008.

"Football is one thing they are watching together," said attorney Herbst, "as they are slowly prepared for a 'normal life' in freedom."

One afternoon, Rosemarie Fritzl quietly slipped out of the Mauer clinic to drive to Ybbsstrasse 40, accompanied by a plainclothes female police officer. It was the first time she had been back to her house since her husband's dungeon had been exposed, and she had been granted police permission to enter, necessary because it was still officially a crime scene.

Dressed in a pale blue blouse and beige slacks, she arrived with the officer in a battered red VW Golf car. Police, on twenty-four-hour guard outside, opened the garden gates for them to drive through. Then, as she walked up to the front door, a group of laughing tourists took her photograph, which would appear in an Austrian newspaper the next morning.

"She had to drive past tourists, laughing and posing in front of the 'House of Horror,'" said a British photographer who witnessed the scene. "It must have been terrible for her. She hurried inside and didn't look back at all."

During her forty-minute visit, she ventured into her husband's notorious cellar for the first time ever, collecting some of Felix's favorite toys and Kerstin's clothes. Then she went upstairs to her old apartment, emerging a few minutes later with two suitcases and a large bag of clothes belonging to Elisabeth and the children, as well as other personal items they'd requested to brighten up their new home.

"It was mentally quite tough for Rosemarie to go back in the house," said a hospital source. "It has become something of a symbol of evil for her. She is, mentally speaking, shattered by the revelations of what happened to her daughter and the charade that her husband acted out for over two decades."

In late June, Elisabeth Fritzl's psychiatrists told prosecutors that she was "too unwell" to make her scheduled court statement in early July. They ruled that she was too traumatized to give evidence from the clinic, even via a video link to St. Polten prison.

Earlier, Elisabeth had asked to give her statement as soon as possible to speed up the legal process. Although her doctors would be there to ensure she was not overwhelmed, the chilling prospect of facing her father, who would be able to challenge her evidence and question her, was proving too much.

Her mother Rosemarie was also due to give evidence at the same hearing, and Kerstin, Stefan and Felix at a later date.

St. Polten's court spokesman Franz Cutka told reporters that the crucial hearing had been put on hold indefinitely, until Elisabeth's doctors deemed her fit enough.

"A video recording of it will be shown at the main trial," he explained. "So the victim will not be required to appear in person to give evidence."

He said preparations for Josef Fritzl's trial were running at "full speed," and Judge Andrea Humer, 48, had been appointed to preside over it. One of her first tasks would be to supervise the taking of Elisabeth's statement.

"We should be able to finalize the charges [in] the early stages by November," said Gerhard Sedlacek, of the prosecutor's office, "with a trial now in the winter months."

After reports surfaced in the Austrian media about

Elisabeth's setback, her attorney Christoph Herbst threatened "judicial steps" against the police and her doctors if they continued to provide information to the media. She now had engaged a second lawyer, Eva Plaz, to protect the family from media intrusion.

In a letter to the authorities, Elisabeth wrote:

> *I require that no data or discussions about what took place in the cellar [is] passed onto any media. It must be the task of the state to prevent exposing that which the Fritzls endured. I want to live in freedom with my children.*

A few days later, Austrian newspapers reported that Josef Fritzl had already started writing his memoirs from his cell, looking to make millions to finance his defense. Elisabeth was said to be "appalled" by the prospect of her father selling his version of the lurid events to the highest bidder.

"It's been bad enough with all the leaks from doctors and police about Elisabeth," said attorney Plaz, "but that her father, who caused all her suffering, means to cash in on her ordeal is sickening."

At the beginning of July, Christa Goetzinger composed a moving tribute song called "24 Years," for her old Amstetten school friend. It was written in the Schlager style that she and Elisabeth had so loved as children.

"24 years"

You were a little girl in a small town,
a girl, with many dreams and wishes
but your fate has chosen someone else
when he took you to the dungeon, at the age of 18.

24 years without love, without luck,
Elisabeth, who's gonna give you back those years?
24 years without light and sunshine
Elisabeth, how long are you gonna stay alone?

Locked like an animal and no way out,
the dungeon was right beneath your parents' house.
Why this particular place, that's obvious
because your father was your tormentor.

24 years without love, without luck,
Elisabeth, who's gonna give you back those years?
24 years without light and sunshine
Elisabeth, how long are you gonna stay alone?

Your new life starts right now, forget the dark past,
we wish you all a lot of luck and bliss,
your look is now focused on the future,
everything will be fine,
we know that you are strong,
just don't lose your courage.

24 years without love, without luck,
Elisabeth, who's gonna give you back those years?
Over, the time without luck and love
Elisabeth, go and get your years back.

"Some people think it should be more hip-hop or more modern," said Christa. "But I wanted to reflect the kind of music we used to share."

And she recorded it with Amstetten-based musician Ighino Veselsky, for a CD to raise money for the family.

Since reading about her best friend's ordeal in the newspapers, Christa, who is now married, had desperately tried to make contact with her old friend. After reading that the family would be adopting new identities, she feared losing contact forever.

So she sent a copy of the CD to the Mauer clinic, along with a letter to Elisabeth.

A few weeks later, Christa received a legal letter from attorney Herbst, ordering her to immediately take the CD off the market, handing over any donations she had received.

"I am very disappointed and I do not understand it," she said. "I thought the legal letter was a bit over the top, but at the end of the day, Elisabeth's well-being is all that counts."

On Friday, July 4, Lisa Fritzl secretly left the clinic, to spend four days "incognito" with 4,000 other children, at the annual youth fire brigade camp. For the first time in almost three months, the 15-year-old was reunited with her school friends she had missed so much.

Local Fire Chief Armin Blutsch told the *Kurier* newspaper in a story headlined, "A Big Step Towards a Normal Life," that she had masked her identity with a false name, and there had been no problems. The paper also reported that other family members had recently made day trips outside the clinic in disguise to go swimming and rambling, and even take a trip to the cinema.

"Fortunately everything is going well," said family lawyer Christoph Herbst, adding that all family members were devoting some time each day to personally answering the hundreds of letters received from well-wishers, from as far away as Australia and China.

CHAPTER 28

Elisabeth Speaks

On Friday, July 11, Elisabeth Fritzl was driven to a secret location to begin three days of filming a video deposition against her father, covering every torturous aspect of her twenty-four-year imprisonment. A doctor and a psychologist would sit with her in a small room, to help her through her ordeal.

Defender Rudolf Mayer and state prosecutor Christine Burkheiser sat in an adjoining room, watching her testimony over a closed-circuit television monitor. They were both able to question her using a microphone. Defendant Josef Fritzl had waived his right to attend his daughter's questioning, remaining in his prison cell.

Judge Andrea Humer, who would be questioning Elisabeth, gave the go-ahead only after doctors told her that Elisabeth was now "in relatively good health," and able to testify.

In "excruciating" detail, she recounted how her father had begun raping her when she was 11, giving more details than she had the night police had first brought her in for questioning.

She described how her father had tricked her into the dungeon, raping her repeatedly for three days while she was handcuffed to a pole.

She also revealed how her father made her watch pornographic movies, then forced her to reenact his favorite parts. And if she ever refused to let him have his way with her, he would punish her and the children by turning off the lights for long periods, and stop bringing in food.

"He was very brutal against me," Elisabeth reportedly told Judge Humer. "And when I did not agree to have sex, then the kids would suffer. We knew he would kick us or be bad to us."

She accused her father of constantly bullying and belittling her and the children, viciously punishing them if they ever dared to answer back.

"It was his kind of communication to use rough words," Elisabeth explained. "He would be insulting against [us]. When he was at the table and we were eating and someone was holding the knife wrongly, or did not want to eat, there would be verbal abuse.

"When he said such words against the kids, they ducked and tried to get out of his way. He would say, 'Shut up and get away from me.' And if that wasn't enough he would become even more abusive."

She told the judge how he refused to even allow the children to develop their own personalities.

"When they were small," she said, "it wasn't such a problem. But as they grew bigger . . . it was more of a problem. He did not like it. He would not allow the kids to have their own will."

Elisabeth also explained how she tried to make the children's daily lives as normal as possible, under the horrific conditions.

"When he went away," she said, "we led our own lives. When he was here it was all silence. We just tried to survive. He was just all-powerful."

Her father would constantly threaten to let them all

rot in the cellar, saying that without him they had no chance of survival.

"He said he could close the door whenever he wanted," she said, "and then we would see how [long] we survived."

Then Judge Humer asked if she had taken his threats seriously.

"Yes," sobbed Elisabeth.

Perhaps most damning of all, she reiterated her assertion that her father was directly responsible for 3-day-old Michael's 1997 death, through neglect, a claim prosecutors hoped would bring a murder charge.

"He is the killer of my son," Elisabeth testified.

Also present, listening carefully to her testimony, was a neonatologist (an expert in baby deaths), hired by the prosecution to render an expert opinion as to whether the unhealthy dungeon conditions had caused Michael's death.

"If it emerges that Fritzl was aware that the child was severely ill," said prosecution spokesman Gerhard Sedlacek, "and he did nothing to get medical help, that would be a case of murder under negligence, and he would be charged accordingly."

Two weeks after Elisabeth's testimony, Kerstin and Stefan both refused to testify against their father. This was a major setback for prosecutors, who needed their testimony to shore up the murder case against Fritzl.

"It is not clear when or if the two adult children will be questioned," Sedlacek told reporters. "It now appears possible that they could use their right not to make any statements."

Prior to Elisabeth's video deposition, prosecutors had considered the two cellar children's testimony crucial for their case against him, for Fritzl now faced a manslaughter charge, in addition to rape, abuse, incarceration and incest. But without any forensic evidence, prosecutors believed the first two charges would be difficult to prove. And unlike the American legal system, Austrian law does not allow cumulative sentences, meaning he could receive just one sentence and be a free man in ten years.

But after Elisabeth's strong testimony, prosecutors decided Stefan and Kerstin's testimonies would no longer be necessary.

Chief Inspector Franz Polzer said Elisabeth had provided "a mountain of evidence" against Fritzl, sparing Stefan and Kerstin the ordeal of testifying.

"There will be no need to make the children, who are already desperately scarred, talk about what happened," he told reporters, "as this could trigger flashbacks and posttraumatic stress."

Less than a month after moving into the new villa, Elisabeth Fritzl ordered her mother Rosemarie to leave and never come back. She was reportedly furious that her three children raised upstairs were still calling Rosemarie "Mom."

According to press reports, in the three months since they had been reunited, Elisabeth had begun asking her mother certain questions, and tensions had been growing. She wanted to know why Rosemarie had been so passive during her fifty-two-year marriage to Josef Fritzl, not leaving him in 1967 after his rape conviction.

She was also angry that her mother had done nothing to protect her, after he'd started raping her as a child. Finally, she began to ask how her mother had never been suspicious of the cellar while living upstairs.

Rosemarie was said to be "shattered" at being thrown

out of the family's new home with no money. In desperation, the frail 69-year-old went to Linz, moving in with another daughter, until she could get herself back on her feet.

Family lawyer Christoph Herbst confirmed that she had left the family home, denying that Elisabeth had ordered her to leave.

"If you run away from your past," said Herbst cryptically, "you will forever be on the run."

A few days after being evicted, Rosemarie was seen shopping in Linz. The once-portly grandmother had lost at least 50 pounds, and was now living on $600 a month in state benefits and looking for an apartment.

On Saturday, July 26, she returned to Ybbsstrasse 40, slipping into her old house to move out her possessions. Paparazzi photographed her packing two cars and a trailer with her things, including a chest of drawers, a mattress and a duvet.

On her way out, a neighbor asked how she was doing. "I'm fine, I'm fine," she said, driving off.

Later that afternoon, a large moving truck arrived to collect the rest of her belongings, including a dresser, couch and assorted pieces of furniture.

"My sister has totally lost it," Rosemarie's sister Christine told a Swedish newspaper. "She is also a victim, and cannot understand [why] she does not get any help from anyone."

Three days later, Rosemarie announced she would divorce her husband after the trial, reverting to her maiden name. It was reported that Elisabeth had demanded it.

Within hours of her announcement, the *Osterreich* newspaper ran a story saying that Josef Fritzl may have raped one of Rosemarie's sisters (not Christine), many years earlier. Investigators had reportedly found an old diary among thousands of his papers, hidden deep in a bolted room in the cellar, with an entry proudly describing the horrific rape.

A few days later, the police said they were considering whether to flood the cellar with reinforced liquid concrete, so it could never be turned into a ghoulish money-making museum.

"No one from that family," said Christoph Herbst, "will ever want to live in that house again."

On Sunday, August 3, prosecutors announced that they were considering charging Josef Fritzl with slavery, under an ancient unused Austrian law. Fearful that under the Austrian legal system he could walk away with a minimal 10-year sentence, a top legal expert had suggested the slavery charge, in addition to possible manslaughter and murder ones.

If prosecutors decided to go down the slavery road, Josef Fritzl would become the first person in Austrian history to be charged under the obscure paragraph 104 of the 19th century Austrian Penal Code, outlawing slavery, which carries a 20-year sentence. This would ensure that the 73-year-old defendant stayed behind bars for the rest of his life.

Two weeks after Elisabeth Fritzl's testimony, prosecutors were finding the country's highest ever criminal profile case riddled with problems. The manslaughter or murder charges, relating to baby Michael's death, could easily be derailed by the lack of any forensic evidence in the thirteen years since his death. The rape charge was also thought to be problematical, if Elisabeth testified she did not fight him off during her twenty-four-year incarceration. The only firm charge was incest, which could see him released in just a few years.

Now top Austrian politicians were demanding that Fritzl receive a far stiffer punishment to fit his terrible crimes.

Judge Kurt Leitzenberger, of St. Polten Regional Court, where the eventual trial would take place, told the London *Times* that there was no legal precedent in Austrian history for the Fritzl case.

"Compiling the charges against the subject is a delicate procedure for a number of reasons," said the judge, "and prosecutors are carefully examining all possibilities."

At the beginning of August, there were reports that Elisabeth Fritzl had been seen taking long romantic walks in the Mauer clinic gardens with a tall, handsome ponytailed man in his thirties. There were even reports of a romance.

"He doesn't dress like a doctor," a source inside the clinic told the London *Daily Star.* "He looks more like a heavy metal fan. They spend a lot of time talking together."

A few days later, Elisabeth secretly brought Kerstin, Stefan and Felix back to the cellar dungeon, to help investigators build their case against their father. The police wanted the former captives to take them through their daily routine, to get a better idea of how they'd lived and what they'd done in their subterranean jail.

It was a highly emotional visit, and a team of psychiatrists accompanied them, to help them through the ordeal.

Later, Elisabeth took her six children to a surprise tea party at Ulmerfeld-Hausmening police headquarters, seven miles outside Amstetten, to thank officers for all the hard work they had done on behalf of the family. She baked a large cake for the occasion, and

presented the officers with a special thank-you poster
for protecting them.

On the red poster, illustrated by the family, was a
centipede with family members' names on it, and a
foam-rubber butterfly.

A handwritten message on the poster read:

*We would like to thank you for your constant
sympathy and protection. You stood with us during the first, very hard times and made us feel
safe and strong.*

Ulmerfeld-Hausmening Police Chief Karl Gschoepf
said he had known nothing about it until Elisabeth arrived with her children, bearing a gift basket including
several bottles of wine.

"It was such a shock," he said. "The children had
painted a very touching picture, and she brought a deli-
cious cake. We also had coffee and ice cream, and just
sat around and chatted."

Elisabeth gave a short speech, thanking the officers,
and saying how happy she was to be with "normal people" again.

"The entire family, including the eldest girl, seemed
strong," said Chief Gschoepf. "You would never guess
what Elisabeth has been through. She is an extremely
strong, courageous woman, who does everything for
her children without worrying about herself."

Elisabeth had impressed everyone by her strength
and devotion to her children, since they'd come out of
the cellar.

"She is an extremely strong, settled woman," he
said, "who cares for her children impressively."

Chief Gschoepf, whose men guarded the family at

the clinic, said the high-profile case had put great pressure on everybody.

"We had no idea what state the family and the mother would be in," he said, "and whether they would accept us. We were with them constantly and felt with them. It was a dramatic experience for us as well."

Just how well Elisabeth and the downstairs children were recovering was a matter of debate. Since the family hired attorney Eva Plaz to handle media relations, highly positive stories of their progress had regularly appeared in the Austrian press.

According to one widely published report, Elisabeth was teaching her three cellar children to swim, run and skate. It was said that Elisabeth and the children were now racing around the grounds of the Mauer clinic on rollerblades, startling patients and staff.

"They're always overtaking people walking in the grounds, [who] usually have no idea who they are," said clinic official Fritz Lengauer.

But a few days later, the daily Austrian newspaper *Osterreich* carried another report, asking, "How Bad Are the Fritzl Victims Really?" This story claimed that Elisabeth and her three downstairs children were faring far worse than previously thought, and were being heavily sedated with tranquilizers, to help them forget their nightmare in the cellar.

It claimed that Kerstin was suffering from serious posttraumatic stress disorder, similar to what Vietnam veterans encountered when they returned to America. Since emerging from her coma, she had allegedly suffered devastating panic attacks, brought on by the slightest thing, like a closing door, a small room or a light being turned off.

The bombshell story also revealed how the terrible

conditions in the cellar had driven Kerstin to tear out her hair and rip her dresses into shreds, before throwing them in the toilet and blocking it, just as Josef Fritzl had complained about in his jailhouse statement.

A family friend was quoted as saying that the 19-year-old had "closed the door on many dark things that have happened to her, and she may never be well enough to open it."

According to the report, Stefan was also in a bad state. At 5 feet 9 inches, 3 inches taller than the highest point in the cellar, he still could not walk properly. After more than three months' physiotherapy, he still had serious problems with coordination and his motor skills. He got dizzy when he walked and doctors feared his spine might never straighten, leaving him crippled.

"They are suffering far more than previously thought," reported the newspaper.

The only one of the downstairs children doctors believed would make a complete recovery was Felix, who'd spent far less time down there, and might be able to forget his past nightmare.

Attorney Plaz has told prosecutors that Felix is too young to give evidence against his father, and Kerstin and Stefan are still not ready.

At the beginning of September, Lisa, Monika and Alexander returned to their studies at secret schools around Amstetten. They were said to be looking forward to returning to their studies and meeting their new classmates.

"We wanted a harmonic start in the new school year," explained the Mauer Clinic's security chief, Fritz Lengauer.

A few days later, the neonatologist's report that Josef Fritzl must have been aware of baby Michael's medical condition and could have saved his life was leaked to the Austrian press. And it was widely reported that Fritzl, who had now hired a second lawyer to negotiate a book deal and arrange to turn Ybbstrasse 40 into a ghoulish tourist site and rent out rooms to help finance his defense, would now be charged with manslaughter.

This would be in addition to St. Polten's prosecutor's office's previous announcement that Josef Fritzl will face up to 3,000 rape charges, after admitting having sex with his daughter Elisabeth up to three times a week during her twenty-four-year incarceration.

Prosecutors have now decided that Rosemarie and Elisabeth's six surviving children will not have to testify. But court officials are worried about whether it will be possible to find an impartial jury of eight, with two alternates, as required by Austrian law, with all the intense publicity surrounding the case.

"We are a small country," said a court official. "There can't be ten people out there who don't already have strong opinions about this man and what he's done."

The entire trial will be held in private, except for the opening formalities and sentencing. So the full extent of Josef Fritzl's crimes may never be known.

On Thursday, September 25, Josef Fritzl returned to Ybbstrasse 40, accompanied by Judge Nikolaus Obrovsky and three police officers. He arrived at 9:46 A.M. in a white Volkswagen mini-bus, calmly reading a book, and was photographed being escorted up the drive. In the five months since his arrest, he had visibly aged, losing much weight and most of his hair.

The judge had ordered the visit to allow him to explain his "escape plan" for Elisabeth and the children in the event that anything ever happened to him. And he spent three hours inside the cellar, taking the judge on a guided tour and answering questions about the 660-pound eighth door to the dungeon. Also present were his attorney Rudolf Mayer and prosecutor Christiane Burkheiser, who would say he had acted strangely, constantly referring to himself in the third person.

"He didn't show any emotion," said a neighbor who observed his return. "He talked to the police who were pointing things out in the garden, then they went inside."

A few days later, after Fritzl had reportedly failed to persuade the judge that he had installed any kind of escape mechanism in the dungeon, he accused the police of removing his time-lock so they could increase the charges against him.

EPILOGUE

On Oct. 22, St. Polten court-appointed psychiatrist Heidi Kastner's 130-page report was leaked to the Austrian Press. The result of six long prison interviews, the report revealed that Josef Fritzl now blamed his abusive mother for his behavior.

"I was born to rape," he told Dr. Kastner. "Bearing that in mind, I controlled myself for quite a long time. I could have behaved a lot worse than locking up my daughter."

Fritzl described himself as an "alibi child," claiming his mother had only had him to prove her fertility. He also likened himself to "a volcano"—quiet on the surface, but then "the evil in him would break out" when he could no longer "control his urges."

He complained to Dr. Kastner that his tyrannical mother had neglected him, claiming that as the bombs rained down over Amstetten in the Second World War, she had abandoned him in the family home alone, while she went into a shelter. He also moaned that she had waited years before taking him to the doctor to treat a painful urinary tract illness.

Fritzl also admitted to never being able to look Elisabeth in the face when he raped her, distancing himself from his actions. And that he stopped having sex with his wife, Rosemarie, the very day he imprisoned Elisabeth.

In her summing up, Dr. Kastner found that although Fritzl had profound psychological issues, as well as severe personality and sexual deviancy disorders, he was sane enough to stand trial. But she recommended that he should spend his remaining days in a secure psychiatric unit, and should never be a free man again, as he would always be a danger to society.

"His narcissism," wrote Dr. Kastner, "combined with the lack of empathy and exploitative way of turning others into instruments of satisfying his own needs. There is also a noticeable ability or tendency to 'modify' reality according to his own wishes."

A week later, the Austrian magazine *News* reported that Fritzl had also told Dr. Kastner how he had imprisoned his mother in an upstairs room for over twenty years before her eventual death. According to another batch of leaked court papers, Fritzl was quoted as saying, "I locked her up in a room at the top of the house. I then bricked in the window so that she never again saw the light of day."

The report said that in 1959, after assuming ownership of her Ybbsstrasse 40 home, he had told neighbors that she had died. According to Fritzl, she did not die until 1980, four years before he imprisoned Elisabeth.

But his latest claim seems highly unlikely, as in 1968 he served an 18-month jail sentence, later spending time abroad on his release.

Maria Fritzl's ultimate fate remains a mystery.

On Nov. 13, Josef Fritzl was formally charged with murder, rape, slavery, incest, abuse and imprisonment. The twenty-seven-page indictment accused Fritzl of killing baby Michael in the cellar by failing to get medical help even though "he knew the life-threatening situation of the newborn." It also accused him of subjecting Elisabeth to "multiple attacks," making her completely dependant on him for her survival, giving her no alternative but to provide "sexual services."

His attorney, Rudolf Mayer, said his client would not appeal the charges.

"I realize now that I am not normal," Mayer reported Fritzl as telling him. "With the help of therapists I want to know what the real reasons are for why I behaved like I did. I want to get treatment."

The Josef Fritzl case is so disturbingly unique that in order to gain some insight into the depths of his dark mind, and his possible motivations, I consulted the highly respected forensic psychiatrist Keith Ablow, M.D., known to millions for his novels and true crime books, including a bestselling book called *Inside the Mind of Scott Peterson*. He also hosts a daily syndicated talk program, *The Dr. Keith Ablow Show*, and is a Fox News contributor.

"The kind of things from which I draw a psychological profile," Dr. Ablow explained, "are really about things of one's family of origin and culture."

Dr. Ablow, while emphasizing that he would never hazard a complete diagnosis of Josef Fritzl without a deeper exploration of his psyche, including an interview, believes two events in his past may have led to this tragedy—his childhood in Nazi Germany and his relationship with his mother.

"If it's the case that his mother seduced him and they actually had sex," said Dr. Ablow, "or it was a kind of unrealized but very powerful seduction, then that can become a determining factor for a young person, as he develops psychosexually."

The doctor says Fritzl's abhorrent behavior in later life could possibly be explained by boyhood Oedipal fantasies involving his mother.

"It can be the case that his imprisoning his own child and hiding her," said Dr. Ablow, "while creating a family with her, is a pathologic outgrowth of something in his own psyche. So you could see the imprisonment and burial of her, and the actual sexual acts with her, and even creating a family with her in secret, as a real-life expression of his psychosexual fantasies as a boy.

"So he's become the mother and actualized what did not occur. One could say his childhood wish to raise a family with a parent in secret, as such impulses generally are, resulted in him doing it in the real world, behind very thick walls."

Dr. Ablow also found significance in Fritzl's statement of being as strong as his mother, and therefore able to control his lustful desires for her.

"Those desires come from somewhere," noted the doctor. "And most boys' Oedipal feelings are not so consciously powerful as to require them to resist day in and day out, and consider themselves very strong because they didn't have sex with their mothers. That's a highly unusual assessment of oneself."

Fritzl's powerful sexual attraction to his mother must have been fed by something, possibly her crossing into improper boundaries when he was a boy. And any subsequent deep psychological damage caused, if left unexplored and unhealed, could remain dormant for a while—but not forever.

"It can manifest itself in later years," explained the doctor, "when he is sideswiped or overcome by, or becomes this dark fantasy. He takes six years to construct his fantasy eventually, in which time he isn't the vulnerable one, he is the one caging the child. And so that's the way really dark psychological dramas play out. They go away, underground, unaddressed."

Particularly significant is his early history of exposing himself to women, before progressing to violent rape.

"It may tell us he has a history of some sexual trauma," said Dr. Ablow. "And I think those things are relevant. It goes along with the psychological picture that if he felt disempowered as a young person by this manipulative, controlling mother, who maybe took things from him sexually that she shouldn't have—whether his desires or the physical act itself—and then as an extension of that fantasy, he takes his own daughter.

"Up to that point he's been caging women, whether insisting that they look at him naked when they don't want to, or raping one at knifepoint, for which he was caught. He may have raped more than one, because getting caught your first time maybe isn't so common. And then he caged his daughter, when the original thing that he references, which is interesting, is that he wanted to cage his mother."

Dr. Ablow also thinks the political backdrop of Nazi Germany, unfolding behind his dark psychic fantasies, could have helped fuel them. He finds it relevant that Fritzl grew up in the shadows of the Mauthausen death camp in Amstetten, while feeling imprisoned by his mother and fighting his Oedipal desires.

Dr. Ablow likens it to the famous M. C. Escher drawing of two hands drawing each other.

"I would venture that whatever was happening in that death camp had its mirror image in what was happening in his personal life," said Dr. Ablow. "I think that he lived within a half mile of the death camp, in an environment that felt to him like a death camp, led to him creating something not unlike it for his offspring.

"And that is the backdrop against which the man develops—the smoke of the crematorium echoing, or perhaps for his own slow death in whatever oven represented his childhood."

The doctor sees the vampires of literature as a fitting metaphor for Josef Fritzl.

"He is a dead man," said Dr. Ablow. "He is feasting on the emotional lives of others, because he lacks that core empathy and emotion himself. And the way you get to be a vampire is that you get bitten by another one. So that the question is in part: Who was the vampire that bit him? Who turned him into the living dead?"

The doctor thinks Fritzl may have selected Elisabeth as his wife and the mother of his downstairs family, seeing some part of her that he was missing.

"You wonder if she was especially sensitive," he said. "Whether she represented something that he lacked, and therefore wanted to imprison it. And yet paradoxically he reproduces it, intuitively at some level. It has real value as regards goodness, that he doesn't have himself.

"So I wouldn't be surprised if she had some magical, emotional, intuitive quality that he found destructive, because he doesn't have it, and therefore wanted to lock it up.

"Nothing comes from nowhere," Ablow said. "Everything that [Josef Fritzl] did will ultimately be explained by what he experienced in his life."